CLASSIC EPHEMERA

CLASSIC EPHEMERA

Compiled by

Darren Henley and Tim Lihoreau

First published 2009 by Elliott and Thompson Limited
27 John Street, London WC1N 2BX
www.eandtbooks.com

ISBN 978-1-9040-2781-2

A CIP catalogue record for this book is available from the British Library.

Printed and bound in the UK by CPI Mackays, Chatham ME5 8TD

FOREWORD

by Howard Goodall

I was invited to join the Classic FM team in the spring of 2008, as presenter of a weekly Saturday afternoon show and, in due course, as Composer-in-Residence. What has taken me by surprise in my year of presenting *Howard Goodall On...* each week (for which I choose and research my own music choices) is how much I would learn in the process.

I thought I knew my classical music trivia, to a point, but I have been quite taken aback at the wealth of intriguing minutiae that I have uncovered along the way, nuggets of knowledge that definitely weren't on the syllabus of my university music course. It turns out that Classic FM has been unearthing unexpected facts – the kind that bring a smile to your face – all along, and I am merely Johnny-come-lately on a quest others have been pursuing for many years, especially Tim Lihoreau and Darren Henley, the authors of this book. It has been a challenge for me to reveal information about composers that *even they* didn't know. It is possible. I note, for instance, with undisguised glee that in the 'composers who share the same birthday' list in this book Tim and Darren have omitted one remarkable double-birthday in the field of musical theatre: Stephen Sondheim and Andrew Lloyd Webber (22nd March, 18 years apart). I share mine with jazz legend Miles Davis, but I wouldn't dare suggest putting my own in amongst the existing illustrious list!

Discovering that Russian composer Alexander Scriabin died from a shaving cut, for example, in my programme about 'sticky endings' or that Armenian composer Khachaturian (he of the 'Sabre Dance') was actually a trained biologist, a fact brought to the surface in my programme on music and science, has given me immense satisfaction, and I'm not embarrassed to admit it.

This collection, to which I feel I may have occasionally but modestly contributed as fellow-traveller, is a kind of QI for music. We composers turn out to upset many preconceptions about us as tormented, ill-tempered loners, battling with an exasperated landlord, a long-suffering patron, or an inebriated conductor (though all of these confrontations have also occurred). We have foibles. We develop strange superstitions and routines and many of us – contrary to the popular view of us as obsessively single-minded – have other interests, hobbies and fascinations. Apart from Borodin's professional achievements as a research chemist, Rossini's eminence as a *chef de cuisine* or Paderewski's becoming Prime Minister of Poland, there's Gerald Finzi, an English composer of the early 20th century, who was a serious apple grower and cider-brewer: indeed, without his extensive orchards, some rare varieties of British apple would otherwise have become extinct by now. This is what one might call core repertoire.

In a written answer to a question from a reader of the Soviet newspaper *Pravda*, composer Prokofiev once actually *worked out* the mathematical equation that would reveal when composers had exhausted all possible combinations of notes in their works. I love this kind of anecdote; it tells me much more about Prokofiev than that he went – with thousands of others – to study at the St. Petersburg Conservatoire. His death was also on the same day as Stalin's, going virtually unreported as a consequence, in case you were interested. If the word 'anorak' is lurking at the back of your diaphragm on hearing these pieces of research, resist its lure and choke it back, since, surely, life's richness is captured in the subtle details of the tapestry.

If on the other hand you are still ruminating over that calculation of Prokofiev's, then admit it, you're hooked, aren't you? Well, it starts with the bewildering proposition that each melody of 8 notes is made up of 6 million alternatives. I am hoping that 70 years since he wrote that, there are still a few left for the likes of me. If not, there's always that old cider press in the barn...

INTRODUCTION

Since we first turned on our transmitters, all of us at Classic FM have believed that classical music should be a part of everyone's life. If you already listen to the music we play every day and you want to know more about it, then you've come to the right place.

This may not be the biggest book about classical music that you'll be able to find. But what it lacks in size, it makes up for in facts, stories and, most important of all, recommendations for great music to listen to.

As we put together our radio programmes, we often discover fascinating facts and titillating titbits about the world of classical music. After many years of collecting this information, we've gathered it all together here in one single book, which spans composer biographies, instrument profiles, general trivia, lengthy lists and quotable sayings. This is the result.

So if you're hoping to uncover the killer fact to spice up your after-dinner conversation; if you want to dazzle your friends with your knowledge of the stories behind the greatest classical music; or if, like us, you're simply an acquirer of trivia, we hope there will be something for you in the next 180 or so pages.

If you haven't listened to Classic FM yet, then hopefully this book will well and truly whet your appetite, as well as answering some of the questions about classical music that you've always wanted to ask.

Darren Henley
Tim Lihoreau

A WORD ABOUT CLASSIC FM

Classic FM is the UK's only 100% classical music radio station. Since we began broadcasting in September 1992, the station has brought classical music to millions of people across the UK. If you've yet to discover for yourself the delights of being able to listen to classical music 24 hours a day, you can find Classic FM on 100-102 FM, on DAB Digital Radio, online at www.classicfm.com, on Sky channel 0106 and on Virgin Media channel 922.

Classic FM Magazine is published monthly, containing full details of the station's programming, as well as the latest news and interviews from the world of classical music. A free CD accompanies each month's magazine, which is available from most newsagents.

Among Classic FM's many CD releases is a new range exclusively available from HMV. The *Classic FM Full Works* series provides top quality recordings of many of the most popular classical works, played in full by world famous musicians. Priced at just £5.99, these CDs are perfect for both the dedicated collector and for those who are just discovering classical music. You can find out more at www.classicfm.com/fullworks.

Classic FM works particularly closely with five orchestras around the UK, with the aim of encouraging new listeners to enjoy the power and passion of hearing a live orchestra playing in the concert hall. Check the station's website to find out if the Royal Scottish National Orchestra, Northern Sinfonia, the Royal Liverpool Philharmonic Orchestra, the Philharmonia Orchestra or the London Symphony Orchestra are performing near you.

> *For changing people's manners and altering their customs there is nothing better than music.*
> **SHU CHING, 600 B.C.**

MUSICAL ERAS

Any music that was composed before 1600 is said to be from the **Early** or **Renaissance** period. Gregorian chant falls into this category (named after Pope Gregory who did much to develop church music), lots of which is very beautiful and relaxing.

Music written between, roughly, 1600 and 1750 is described as coming from the **Baroque** period. Composers who were producing new material at this time include Bach, Handel and Vivaldi.

Now, here's a funny one. Everything we play on Classic FM is classical music. But anything written between roughly 1750 and 1830 is described as coming from the **Classical** period. This includes the work of Haydn and Mozart. Beethoven, too, wrote some music in the classical period but he also stayed on after the bell had gone for the early Romantic period and wrote some stuff in that one too.

Love features heavily in classical music, just as it does in pop. But, when we are talking about eras, **romantic** refers to the composers who were writing music from roughly 1830 to 1910, including Schubert, Chopin and Berlioz.

Modern music is another odd one. Anything written after the early 1900s is generally referred to as coming from the Modern period, despite the fact that some of it is now more than a hundred years old. A car of equivalent age would be vintage. In time, we may come to call it '20th and 21st Century' music, to allow for stuff written after the year 2000.

If you imagine that eras in music are like star signs, with **Modern** as Aquarius (genius or mad, hard to tell), **Romantic** as Cancer (slushy, doe-eyed, dreamy) and **Classical** as Gemini (sometimes slushy, sometimes not), then **Baroque** is clearly the Virgo – neat, tidy, everything in its place, but never too much emotion.

1

FIVE LINES THAT CHANGED THE WORLD

One of the great unsung heroes of classical music – in fact, all music – is Guido D'Arezzo. He was the clever chap who came up with the five lines on which almost all music is now written, called a 'stave'. He thought of it at more or less the same time as somebody in China invented gunpowder.

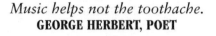

Music helps not the toothache.
GEORGE HERBERT, POET

OPUS

The Italian word for 'work', used, simply, to put together a database of a composer's work in chronological order. So *Opus 3* would be the third piece (or a part of the third piece) that a composer had written. Opus numbers tend to follow the published date of a work, not necessarily the date the composer wrote it. Hence, Chopin's published *Piano Concertos No. 1* and *No. 2* were actually written in the order 2 and 1 (see page 60). Mozart and J.S. Bach have their own numbering systems. Mozart's was done by Ludwig von Köchel, who, being a shy and retiring sort of chap, decided to give each of Mozart's works a Köchel number instead of an Opus number. In J.S. Bach's case, his pieces all have *BWV* in front of the number. These initials stand for 'Bach Werke-Verzeichnis', which is German for 'Catalogue of Bach's Works', and are not, as some think, a 'best before' date mark.

Check out: Three great numbers to learn are: Beethoven's *Opus 67*, Mozart's *K622*, and Tchaikovsky's *Opus 20* – great to drop in at parties. (They are better known as Beethoven's *Symphony No. 5*, Mozart's *Clarinet Concerto* and Tchaikovsky's *Swan Lake*).

OLDEST ORCHESTRA

According to the *Guinness Book of World Records,* the very first symphony orchestra was the Gewandhaus Orchestra, which began playing in Leipzig, Germany, in 1743.

" *Why should the devil have all the good tunes?*
**ROWLAND HILL, INVENTOR OF THE
'PENNY BLACK' STAMP** "

" *You have Van Gogh's ear for music.*
BILLY WILDER, FILM DIRECTOR AND WRITER "

*Cedric's previous job as a percussionist came back to haunt him as one
more beef stroganoff slid to the restaurant floor.*

THE INSTRUMENTS OF THE ORCHESTRA

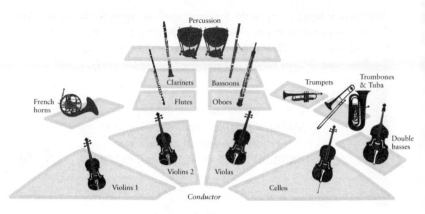

Imagine. Four different types of instruments – some thirty string players alone, as well as ten or so brass, around the same number of woodwind and a liberal sprinkling of percussionists. Seventy-odd different players in all, spread out over a space the size of a tennis court, being told what to do by a guy (or girl) who needn't ever have played a note in his (or her) life. Shouldn't work, should it? But it does. Amazingly.

The human windmill waving the stick in front of the orchestra is the conductor. A passable conductor can be the difference between a bad and a good performance. A great conductor can be the difference between a good and an unforgettable one. (Every now and again in the papers, you will see reviews of concerts where a 'golden silence' occurred at the end of a work, when everyone was just too overwhelmed to start clapping). If you can't quite work out exactly what it is that conductors do, imagine them in the same category as those seemingly imperceptible tights for women which support the bottom – without them, things tend to go pear-shaped.

The illustration above shows how orchestras are conventionally set out on stage, although conductors are free to indulge in a game of musical chairs and move everyone around if they so wish.

CHANGING THE HILDEGARD

Hildegard of Bingen, one of the foremost early composers, not to mention one of the very few famous women composers, wasn't born in Bingen. Nor did she live or die in Bingen. She was actually from Rupertsberg, just down the road. Maybe Bingen just rolled off the tongue easier.

*Military justice is to justice what
military music is to music.*
GROUCHO MARX, ACTOR AND WRITER

A LICENCE TO PRINT MONEY

The English composers Thomas Tallis and William Byrd became rich men when Queen Elizabeth I granted them the exclusive right to print sheet music and manuscript paper in England for 21 years from 1575.

*The good singer should be nothing but
an able interpreter of the ideas of the master,
the composer. In short, the composer and the
poet are the only true creators.*
GIOACHINO ROSSINI, COMPOSER

Sopranos are the highest female voices, providing not only the female lead but also, more often than not, the love-interest for the male tenors in opera. Sopranos often heard on Classic FM include Maria Callas, Renée Fleming, Lesley Garrett, Anna Netrebko and Angela Gheorghiù. **Mezzo-sopranos**, such as Cecilia Bartoli, have voices that are slightly deeper.

Altos are usually female singers who either can't sing as high as sopranos, or who can but want a quiet life, free from throat strain. Just as violas are the slightly lower, some would say duller, versions of violins, so the altos are... well, let's leave it there, shall we? Men can be altos too, but... well, again, let's just leave it there.

Tenors are generally the 'heroes' of the opera world, getting many of the best male arias. The most well-known are *The Three Tenors* – José Carreras, Placido Domingo and the late Luciano Pavarotti – a trio who became multi-millionaires on the back of their stadium concerts around the globe.

Baritones are male singers whose voices are higher than basses, but lower than tenors. So if you can't reach the high notes and have only ever been able to get the low notes first thing in the morning, best become a baritone. The international superstar Bryn Terfel is a fine example of a **bass-baritone**, whose voice, predictably, lies somewhere between a bass and a baritone.

The **basses** are the lowest of the male singers, the ones who sound like they've just got up after a heavy night on the sauce. In opera, they don't get as many of the hero roles as the tenors: if this seems unfair, listen to Lee Marvin singing in *Paint your Wagon* and ask yourself – would you elope with him? Incidentally, bass is pronounced 'base'. Again, quite apt if you remember Lee Marvin's character.

The girls aren't the only ones who can sing high in classical music. **Counter-tenors**, such as James Bowman or Andreas Scholl, have voices that are higher than tenors. However, they hit the high notes without having had to resort to surgery. This was not the case with **castrati**, who were castrated to ensure that their voices never broke. The practice was worryingly fashionable in the 18th century, when the desire for a voice which was a cut above meant a cut below. Castrati were even resident in the Vatican. Alessandro Moreschi, who died in 1922, was the last known castrato and became rather famous in the process. He was the director of the Sistine Chapel Choir in Rome. Nowadays, we're all for loving music, but castration really is a snip too far.

If you hear somebody talking about a singer, no matter what type their voice, or whether they are male or female, performing an *aria,* this basically means they are singing a 'song'. Most of the big hits from operas are arias. They are the solos or set pieces performed by singers playing the big roles.

There is a simple way to spot a singer from among a crowd of other classical musicians: they will be obsessed about protecting their throat and so will be wearing a scarf tied tightly around their necks in even the most sub-tropical of summery conditions. They are also often to be seen carrying bundles of sheet music under their arms, as they take any opportunity to learn their part for their next performance.

66

*One should try everything once,
except incest and folk-dancing.*
ARNOLD BAX, COMPOSER

99

𝄞

GIOVANNI DA PALESTRINA (1525–1594)

The composer Palestrina wasn't called Palestrina. Sorry to shock you, but it's true. His name was Giovanni Pierluigi. He became known as Giovanni da Palestrina – John from Palestrina – because that was the small town near Rome which he called home.

Palestrina's *Missa Papae Marcelli* – literally 'the Mass for Pope Marcellus' – was never actually listened to by its dedicatee. Pope Marcellus reigned for a mere 55 days before he died, never having got around to hearing the piece that carries his name.

Check out: the *Missa Brevis* – a small and perfectly formed place to start.

7

OPERA

Operas tend to be big on great tunes, passion, sorrow, romance and drama. Sadly, they are rarely big on plot. Opera storylines tend to centre around either unrequited love, or bizarre 'what-do-you-mean-you're-really-a-horse-in-disguise?' madness. Broadly speaking though, most opera storylines go something like this: Man falls in love with woman. Woman turns out to be either related or someone she claimed not to be. Man and woman's love doomed. Cue angst (in song). Woman (can be man – doesn't matter) dies horrific death, preferably involving consumption. Remaining lover dies. Big song. The end. Everyone goes down the pub.

In fact, opera is really what classical music would be like if Quentin Tarantino had invented it. But despite the high body count, it has given us some of the most spectacular and beautiful pieces anywhere in classical music. You will find the potted plots of ten famous operas spread throughout the pages of this book.

10 DONS IN OPERA

Don Alfonso .... Donizetti: *Lucrezia Borgia*
Don Alvaro .... Verdi: *La Forza del Destino*
Don Basilio .... Rossini: *The Barber of Seville*
Don Carlos .... Rameau: *Les Indes Galantes*
Don Curzio .... Mozart: *The Marriage of Figaro*
Don Fernando .... Beethoven: *Fidelio*
Don Giovanni .... Mozart: *Don Giovanni*
Don José .... Bizet: *Carmen*
Don José Martinez .... Delius: *Koanga*
Don Quixote .... Purcell: *Don Quixote*

*In opera, anything that is too stupid
to be spoken is sung.*
VOLTAIRE, PHILOSOPHER

SINGING FOR YOUR SUPPER

The Austro-Hungarian Emperor Leopold II loved the premiere of Cimarosa's opera *The Secret Marriage* so much that he invited the whole cast and orchestra to dinner, before demanding that they stage the whole performance from beginning to end once again.

RECORD BREAKER

The biggest selling classical CD of all time is *The Three Tenors Live in Concert*, which was recorded live in Rome in 1990.

THREE TENORS CONCERTS

How many *Three Tenors* concerts do you think were? Two? Three maybe? Think again.

Rome – July 7, 1990
Monte Carlo – June 9, 1994
Los Angeles – July 16, 1994
Tokyo – June 29, 1996
London – July 6, 1996
Vienna – July 16, 1996
New York – July 20, 1996
Gothenburg – July 26, 1996
Munich – August 23, 1996
Düsseldorf – August 24, 1996
Vancouver – December 31, 1996
Toronto – January 4, 1997
Melbourne – March 1, 1997
Miami – March 8, 1997
Modena – June 17, 1997
Barcelona – July 13, 1997
Paris – July 10, 1998
Tokyo – January 9, 1999
Pretoria - April 18, 1999
Detroit - July 17, 1999
San Jose – December 29, 1999
Las Vegas – April 22, 2000
Washington – May 7, 2000
Cleveland – June 25, 2000
São Paulo – July 22, 2000
Chicago – December 17, 2000
Seoul – June 22, 2001
Beijing – June 23, 2001
Yokohama – June 27, 2002
Saint Paul – December 16, 2002
Columbus – September 28, 2003

TENOR AT THE MOVIES

When you're famous for one thing, it can seem like a good idea to try your hand at something else, to see if you can become celebrated for that too. So it was, in 1982, for Luciano Pavarotti when he made an ill-fated bid to achieve stardom as a film actor. Pavarotti played the male lead role in a romantic comedy with the unlikely title, *Yes, Giorgio*. The movie told the tale of an international opera star, by the name of Fini, who suddenly loses his voice. Thanks to the medical expertise and love of a young lady doctor, called Pamela, his vocal cords perk up and all is well in the world. Pavarotti's character is heard to utter a chat up line that deserves to achieve immortality: 'Pamela, you are a thirsty plant. Fini can water you'. *The New York Times* review of the film notes: '*Yes, Giorgio* is rated PG ("Parental Guidance Suggested"). Its sexual innuendoes will not disturb children, although adults may find them alarming.'

CROSSOVER CLASSICAL MUSIC

The boundaries of what is, and what isn't, classical music can sometimes become quite blurred. A singer might have a selection of popular operatic arias in his repertoire, which he sings in an operatic style. These fall comfortably into the definition of being classical music and, although he does not perform in full operas, we would be happy to agree that this is genuine classical music. But at the same time, a singer might also perform what are essentially pop songs in an operatic style. This definitely doesn't make them opera and they shouldn't really be thought of as classical music in its strictest sense. However, many crossover performers have enjoyed huge success in selling records and at getting audiences along to large-scale live concerts. For many people, they offer a route into listening to classical music, and they should hold no threat to the core classical music world. Crossover classical music comes at the point where pop music and classical music collide. Sometimes it doesn't quite work, but sometimes this fusion can create quite a stir.

> *The opera house is an institution differing from other lunatic asylums only in the fact its inmates have avoided official certification.*
> **ERNEST NEWMAN, MUSIC CRITIC**

CHART TOPPER

When the Salford-born tenor, Russell Watson, released his first album *The Voice* in 2001, it topped the UK's classical music chart for an entire year until the release of his second album, *Encore*, which replaced *The Voice* in the top spot.

INSTRUCTIONS

The Italian word **adagio** is a composer's way of telling a performer to play their music slowly. It is slower than **andante** but faster than **largo**. Slow movements, in general are often simply called 'adagios' because so many bear this marking.

At the other end of the scale, **allegro** is another instruction from a composer to a performer. The message is to play fast – not, however, as fast as **presto** but faster than **allegretto** (which means allegro-ish). Probably the most famous allegro of all is the 'da da da DER...' of Beethoven's *Symphony No. 5*.

Allegro is not to be confused with Allegri or the Austin Allegro. The first is a composer born in the 16th century, best known for his choral masterpiece *Miserere*. The second is a 1970s car often favoured by aunties and geography teachers. Paradoxically neither of these groups is exactly renowned for being fast.

Legato is another order composers like to issue to musicians – this time they are asking the performer to play smoothly. The opposite is **staccato** – a rather spikier sound.

So why are all these instructions in Italian? Well, Italy was once the centre of the music industry and therefore all the composers wrote their directions in Italian. This continues today, meaning that a German composer writing for a Spanish pianist and a Dutch violinist would still tell them what speed to play in Italian. Odd, but true.

> *We're not worried about writing for posterity. We just want it to sound good right now.*
> **DUKE ELLINGTON, COMPOSER**

Allegri's glorious *Miserere* was written for the Sistine Chapel Choir in Rome. The Pope declared the music to be so powerful that the score was closely guarded in case anyone else tried to copy the music. It's said that when the young Wolfgang Amadeus Mozart heard the *Miserere* performed during a visit to the chapel, he rushed home and wrote it out in full from memory.

> *Singers have the most marvellous breath control and can kiss for about ten minutes.*
> **JILLY COOPER, NOVELIST**

JOHANN PACHELBEL (1653–1706)

One of classical music's One-Hit-Wonders, this organist and composer is famous for his *Canon.* Just like Albinoni's *Adagio,* it only became mega-well-known more than a couple of hundred years after it was written. But, unlike Albinoni, at least it was all his own work. J.S. Bach was a big fan. By the way, in this instance 'canon' has nothing to do with the weapons of war, that are now often used to blast away in time with the music during live outdoor performances of Tchaikovsky's *1812 Overture* in the grounds of stately homes around Britain. No, Pachelbel's *Canon* is an excellent example of a genre of music you probably know from your childhood. Think back to *Frère Jacques* or *London's Burning* – you might have known them as 'rounds' but the basic principles are the same.

> *It is clear that the first specification for a composer is to be dead.*
> **ARTHUR HONEGGER, COMPOSER,**
> ***I AM A COMPOSER* (1951)**

Marc-Antoine Charpentier is the composer behind the Eurovision Song Contest's biggest hit. The *Prelude* to his *Te Deum* is used as the theme music, which is heard at the beginning and end of the annual televisual extravaganza. Some critics believe that it's the only decent work to be heard all evening.

> *Composers shouldn't think too much –*
> *it interferes with their plagiarism.*
> **HOWARD DIETZ, SONG WRITER**

HENRY PURCELL (1659–1695)

Often referred to as the first great English composer, Purcell was an amazing young talent, becoming Organist of Westminster Abbey – a top job – by the time he was 20. Despite the fact that he only lived for another 16 years, he had a busy old time of it, composing every conceivable type of music. The correct way of pronouncing his name is 'Persil' – rather like the washing powder. Please note that although Purcell is a pleasant accompaniment to doing the washing and ironing, there's absolutely no suggestion whatsoever that his music will make your whites brighter at any temperature.

Check out: *'When I am laid in earth'* (known as *'Dido's Lament'*) from *Dido and Aeneas* | the *Rondo* from *Abdelazar* | *Trumpet Tune and Air in D* | *Come Ye Sons of Art*.

Well, I Never! The huge void left after the death of Purcell, not filled until the arrival of Elgar some 200 years later (if you don't count the naturalised Handel), led England to be dubbed 'the land without music'.

TOMASO ALBINONI (1671–1751)

Best known for his *Adagio for Organ and Strings*, even though it was actually written by an Italian professor in 1958 – the same year as Pele scored a hat-trick in the World Cup in Sweden. It was based on only a fragment of the original manuscript. So, Albinoni wrote hundreds of tunes in his lifetime but is now famous for one he didn't write. A bit like jazz musician, Dave Brubeck, and his hit *Take Five*.

Check out: Any of his *Oboe Concertos*.

Name drop: Remo Giazotto, the Italian professor who reworked the *Adagio*.

Hilary first noticed the spider as she approached
a fiendishly difficult recapitulation.

OBOE

A black, wooden instrument that looks a bit like a clarinet with a straw sticking out of the top. It has a more 'nasal' sound than the clarinet, but, played well, can sound utterly beautiful. Played badly, it can bring to mind Sweep from *The Sooty Show* being attacked by geese. Either way, its piercing sound can always be heard through everything else. It's also the instrument you hear before an orchestral concert, playing the note to which all other instruments tune.

Check out: Albinoni: *Oboe Concertos* | Ravel: *Boléro* | Jean Françaix: *The Flower Clock*.

Name drop: A bit like the bassoon, this one – nobody will ever chastise you for not knowing names of oboe players. Maybe keep composer and oboe player Heinz Holliger in reserve, for special occasions.

Well, I Never! A Heckelphone is the name given to the now largely obsolete baritone oboe, invented in 1904 by, not surprisingly, a Mr Heckel.

> *I cannot switch my voice. My voice is not
> like an elevator going up and down.*
> **MARIA CALLAS, SOPRANO**

COR ANGLAIS

The cor anglais, which translates as 'English horn', is one of the less well-known instruments of the orchestra. Many people mistakenly think that it must be part of the brass section. It actually looks like an oversized oboe and resides firmly in the family of woodwind instruments. Anybody who says they can tell it apart from an oboe is either (a) a genius, (b) a liar, or (c) a cor anglais player.

Check out: You can hear the cor anglais playing the main tune in the slow movement of Dvořák's *New World Symphony* and playing the part of the swan in *The Swan of Tuonela* by Sibelius.

Name drop: As with bassoonists, it's not recommended that you actually name any cor anglais players. If you are ever asked to provide details, simply adopt a misty-eyed, far-away look and sigh knowingly.

YOU CAN'T BE GOOD AT EVERYTHING

Albert Einstein was the man who formulated the theory of relativity, who revolutionised our grasp of matters space and time, and even tweaked the Brownian theory of motion. He was also a keen amateur violinist. Once, below the window of his Mercer Street apartment in Princeton, his violin teacher was heard to say, 'Oh for goodness sake, Albert, can't you count?'

> *I know two kinds of audience only –*
> *one coughing and one not coughing.*
> **ARTUR SCHNABEL, PIANIST**

ANTONIO VIVALDI (1678–1741)

Despite the fact that Vivaldi wrote somewhere around 800 different works, his music was rarely played from his death in 1741 right through to the middle of the 20th century, largely due to an astonishing piece of classical vandalism, which saw masses of his manuscripts deliberately locked away for a century or so. He then had something of a comeback and now sits near the top of the list of most-performed Baroque composers. Were there to be a 'Musical Redheads Hall of Fame', he'd be up there with Cilla Black and Mick Hucknall. Even though he was a priest, he used to tour with both a top soprano *and* her sister. Despite his denials, everyone thought that there was more to this threesome than just trio sonatas. And they say blondes have all the fun.

Check out: *Four Seasons* | *'Gloria'* | *'Nulla in Mundo Pax Sincera'*, used in the film *Shine*.

Well, I Never! Despite being born some 500 kilometres away on the other side of the Alps, Vivaldi ended up in the next graveyard along from Mozart in Vienna. Both of them were in paupers' graves.

> *Making music is like making love:*
> *the act is always the same, but each*
> *time is different.*
> **ARTUR RUBINSTEIN, PIANIST**

> *Opera's when a guy gets*
> *stabbed in the back and instead of*
> *bleeding he sings.*
> **ED GARDNER, AMERICAN RADIO PERSONALITY**

VIOLIN

There is safety in numbers if you are a violin player in an orchestra: around twenty to thirty other people sitting next to you playing the same instrument, all following the leader (the one at the front, nearest the conductor). It's another one of those instruments which has been well-serviced by a plethora of composers over the years with big concertos from Mozart, Beethoven, Brahms, Bruch, Mendelssohn and Tchaikovsky. Paganini was an amazing fiddler himself, leaving behind pieces which are still touchstones in virtuosity today.

Name drop: Itzhak Perlman | Yehudi Menuhin | Nigel Kennedy | Nicola Benedetti | Maxim Vengerov | Joshua Bell | Tasmin Little | Anne-Sophie Mutter.

∾ TEN GREAT VIOLIN CONCERTOS ∾
Bruch: *Violin Concerto No. 1*
Mendelssohn: *Violin Concerto*
J.S. Bach: *Double Violin Concerto*
Beethoven: *Violin Concerto*
Sibelius: *Violin Concerto*
Glass: *Violin Concerto*
Tchaikovsky: *Violin Concerto*
Barber: *Violin Concerto*
Elgar: *Violin Concerto*
Brahms: *Violin Concerto*

> *When I composed that, I was conscious of being inspired by God Almighty. Do you think I consider your puny little fiddle when He speaks to me?*
> **LUDWIG VAN BEETHOVEN, COMPOSER, TO A VIOLINIST WHO BELIEVED THAT A PASSAGE WAS IMPOSSIBLE TO PLAY**

TAKING BONEY APART

Evidently Napoleon fancied himself as something of a music critic, telling the composer Cherubini: 'My dear Cherubini, you are certainly an excellent musician; but really your music is so noisy and complicated that I can make nothing of it'. Without missing a beat, came the reply from the composer: 'My dear general, you are certainly an excellent soldier, but in regard to music, you must excuse me if I don't think it necessary to adapt my compositions to your comprehension'. Touché.

GEORG PHILIPP TELEMANN (1681–1761)

When it came to knocking out the tunes, the German Baroque composer Georg Philipp Telemann simply had no equal. The *Guinness Book of Records* lists him as the most prolific composer of all time and experts reckon that he produced more than 3,700 works. Although his contemporary, J.S. Bach, is now regarded as the greater composer, Telemann was undoubtedly the bigger hit while they were both alive. His music was largely forgotten for a century or so after his death, but interest was revived in the early 1900s.

Check out: *Concerto for Trumpet and Strings in D* | *Concerto for Viola and String Orchestra in G* (the first known concerto for viola – but hey, you can't have everything).

Well, I Never! Despite the scale of his output, Telemann had time to understand the importance of blending commerce with his art. He was a pioneer of the idea of publishing his compositions in a magazine aimed at amateur music makers.

JOHANN SEBASTIAN BACH (1685–1750)

This German composer was the most famous of a large musical family. Alongside Handel, he was one of the greatest composers of the Baroque period. He was also an organist and church music master, which is why lots of his works are religious.

When he was only 19, Bach walked from his home in Arnstadt to Lübeck to hear a performance by his favourite composer, Buxtehude. The teenager then walked all the way back to Arnstadt, a total journey of some 420 miles.

If Bach's *Goldberg Variations* send you to sleep, don't worry. That's what the composer intended. Bach wrote the keyboard work for one Count Kayserling, an insomniac at the Dresden Court, who commissioned him to come up with something 'soft and yet a little gay' to help him sleep. The Count's musicians were given the job of playing all 30 variations to him at night. Bach is also noted for writing *Wachet Auf*, which translates as 'Sleepers Awake'.

One of Bach's most famous pieces, his *Air on the G string*, wasn't so called by the composer himself. In fact, it wasn't written to be played on a G string at all. It got this nickname when a 19th century fiddler called August Wilhelmj rearranged it as a bit of a novelty.

Check out: the *Brandenburg Concertos* | *Toccata and Fugue in D minor* (perfect music for Vincent Price in the film *The Phantom of the Opera*) | *Sheep May Safely Graze*.

Well, I Never! Bach was a fan of two things – coffee and numbers. Lots of his pieces play games with numbers, inaudibly. And he wrote a whole cantata about coffee.

BACH AGAIN... AND AGAIN...

The Bach dynasty's influence on classical music through the years should not be underestimated. Johann Sebastian had twenty children of whom Wilhelm Friedemann, Carl Philipp Emmanuel, Johann Christian and Johann Christoph were all composers. As you can see from the list below, Johann Sebastian didn't show terribly much imagination in naming his kids – five of them were called Johann and one Johanna:

Catherina Dorothea Bach (born 1708)
Wilhelm Friedemann Bach (born 1710)
Maria Sophia Bach (born 1713)
Johann Christoph Bach (born 1713)
Carl Philipp Emanuel Bach (born 1714)
Johann Gottfried Bernhard Bach (born 1715)
Leopald Augustus Bach (born 1718)
Christina Sophia Henrietta Bach (born 1723)
Gottfried Heinrich Bach (born 1724)
Christian Gottlieb Bach (born 1725)
Elisabeth Juliana Friederika Bach (born 1726)
Ernestus Andreas Bach (born 1727)
Regina Johanna Bach (born 1728)
Christiana Benedicta Louise Bach (born 1730)
Christiana Dorothea Bach (born 1731)
Johann Christophe Friedrich Bach (born 1732)
Johann August Abraham Bach (born 1733)
Johann Christian Bach (born 1735)
Johanna Carolina Bach (born 1737)
Regine Susanna Bach (born 1742)

BACH HANDLES

Aside from J.S. Bach, music historians have come up with some handy nicknames to tell which of his composer sons are which. C.P.E. Bach is known as the 'Berlin' or 'Hamburg' Bach; J.C. Bach goes under the alias of the 'London' Bach and W.F. Bach is given the moniker of the 'Halle' Bach.

> *Creativity is more than just being different.*
> *Anybody can play weird – that's easy. What's hard*
> *is to be as simple as Bach. Making the simple*
> *awesomely simple, that's creativity.*
> **CHARLES MINGUS, COMPOSER**

PARALLEL LIVES

Bach and Handel were both born in the same year – 1685. Both suffered from cataracts and were treated unsuccessfully by the same British optician.

> *It's easy to play any musical instrument:*
> *all you have to do is touch the right key at the*
> *right time and the instrument will play itself.*
> **JOHANN SEBASTIAN BACH, COMPOSER**

GEORGE FRIDERIC HANDEL (1685–1759)

Handel showed great talent as a youngster, but he had to suffer for his art. He was forced to sneak a small keyboard up to the loft of his house to practise on, because his father wouldn't let him go near a musical instrument.

In a way, he was the Greg Rusedski of classical music. Although he was German, he was considered one of Britain's great composers, after becoming a British citizen. This came to pass when the Elector of Hanover was promoted to the job of being King George I. His music includes opera and instrumental work, but he's probably best known for his great big choral masterpieces, which are still regularly performed up and down the country today.

Handel's *Music for the Royal Fireworks* was written for a display put on by King George II in London's Hyde Park. The music might have proved to be a hit, but the fireworks definitely weren't. That's all except one particular Catherine wheel, which was what you might call a 'direct hit'. It set fire to a wooden tower and caused pandemonium among the crowds.

While he was in Italy, Handel was challenged to a duel – with a difference. The composer Domenico Scarlatti dared him to agree to a 'keyboard duel' – Handel on organ, Scarlatti on harpsichord. The result was a fudge: Handel was declared the better organist, Scarlatti the better harpsichordist.

Check out: *Messiah* | *'Ombra mai fu'* from the opera *Xerxes* | *Zadok the Priest* (used in the film *The Madness of King George*) | *Water Music* | *Arrival of the Queen of Sheba* from the oratorio *Solomon*.

Well, I Never! Handel was reputedly a big chap with an enormous appetite. Indeed, you often see pictures of him with his jacket bursting at the seams. In one restaurant, he booked a table for four and ordered four meals. When the waiter arrived with four feasts and enquired after his other guests, Handel barked at him to put the food down and rapidly gobbled the lot.

ORATORIO

Often staged in a church or cathedral, an oratorio is a religious story set to music and performed by solo singers, a choir and an orchestra. Usually though, the story is told without scenery and costumes – so the event is more of a concert. In the end, it's a bit like opera, only cheaper. Probably the most famous oratorio is *Messiah* by Handel.

Check out: Mendelssohn: *Elijah* | Walton: *Belshazzar's Feast* | And if you're feeling up to a choral bath, Elgar: *The Dream of Gerontius*.

WHOSE HOUSE?

A house in Brook Street, London, just along the road from Claridges, was home to two musical superstars from different eras. Both the classical composer George Frideric Handel and the rock guitarist Jimi Hendrix lived in the same central London pad – although they were resident there a good 200 years apart.

Advice from one pianist to another:
When a piece gets difficult, make faces.
ARTUR SCHNABEL, PIANIST

FIRST TRACKS

The first piece of music to be played on Classic FM, just after six o'clock on the morning of 7th September 1992, was Handel's *Zadok the Priest*. That was followed by Weber's *Invitation to the Dance*.

MASTERS OF THE KING'S/QUEEN'S MUSIC

1625	Nicholas Lanier
1666	Louis Grabu
1674	Nicholas Staggins
1700	John Eccles
1735	Maurice Green
1755	William Boyce
1779	John Stanley
1786	William Parsons
1817	William Shield
1834	Christian Kramer
1848	George Frideric Handel
1870	William George Cusins
1893	Walter Parratt
1924	Edward Elgar
1934	Walford Davies
1942	Arnold Bax
1953	Arthur Bliss
1975	Malcolm Williamson
2004	Peter Maxwell Davies

DOMENICO ZIPOLI (1688–1726)

Until the premiere of Zimmer's *Gladiator*, this organist and composer's main job was to be the chief 'Z' in classical music. He hailed from Naples, but towards the end of his life he got the travel bug and emigrated to Argentina. His one surviving hit is *Elevazione*, which has become a big favourite for Classic FM listeners.

Well, I Never! In the 1970s, twenty odd previously unknown works by Zipoli turned up in Bolivia. (He had been a Jesuit missionary out in Paraguay).

JOSEPH HAYDN (1732–1809)

To say that Haydn was hard-working would be a dramatic understatement. During the 77 years of his life he wrote no fewer than 104 symphonies, more than 80 string quartets, over 50 piano sonatas, at least 24 concertos and 20 operas. And that's without counting the choral and chamber pieces.

When he was a youngster, Haydn was a chorister at St. Stephen's Cathedral in Vienna. He had a fantastic singing voice. So, when his choirmaster suggested that if he had a small operation he would be able to keep his unbroken voice for the rest of his life, the young Joseph liked the sound of the idea. It was only when his horrified father discovered that his son was about to go under the surgeon's knife that the boy was told what the operation would actually entail.

Later in life, Haydn befriended many famous people and when Lord Nelson and Lady Hamilton visited him in 1800, they got on like a house on fire, exchanging gossip and gifts. Haydn had his new mass performed during the visit and the new work gained the nickname of the 'Nelson Mass'.

Very often neglected in favour of his counterparts, Mozart and Beethoven, it is often said that Haydn is a composer you learn to appreciate more with age.

Haydn's *Cello Concerto No. 1* spent 177 years in obscurity. Once composed, it was lost until 1961, when it was found in the Prague National Museum.

Check out: The magnificent choral work *The Creation* | *Symphony No. 94*, known as the *'Surprise Symphony'* because of the deafening chord that comes crashing in after a very quiet opening | *Cello Concertos Nos. 1 & 2* | *The Seasons*.

Name drop: The German National Anthem. Haydn wrote the music, originally as a part of a *String Quartet in C*, and various words were added at later stages.

Joseph Haydn might well have been given the nickname 'Papa Haydn', but if you come across the composer Michael Haydn, then don't be fooled into thinking that it's his son. Michael and Joseph were in fact brothers, with the latter having no children at all.

> ❝ *I don't know much about classical music. For years I thought Goldberg Variations were something Mr and Mrs Goldberg tried on their wedding night.*
> **WOODY ALLEN, FILM ACTOR AND DIRECTOR,**
> ***STARDUST MEMORIES* (1980)** ❞

NICKNAMES OF 10 OF HAYDN'S SYMPHONIES

Symphony No. 22 .... The Philosopher
Symphony No. 55 .... The Schoolmaster
Symphony No. 60 .... The Distraught Man
Symphony No. 82 .... The Bear
Symphony No. 83 .... The Hen
Symphony No. 94 .... Surprise
Symphony No. 100 .... Military
Symphony No. 101 .... Clock
Symphony No. 103 .... Drumroll
Symphony No. 104 .... London

> ❝ *I loathe divas, they are the curse of true music and musicians.*
> **HECTOR BERLIOZ, COMPOSER** ❞

SLOWLY DECOMPOSING

After they died, it took a while for many of the greatest composers to be allowed to rest in peace. Bach, Mozart, Haydn, Beethoven and Schubert were all exhumed and reburied at various times. Mozart, Haydn and Donizetti's skulls were also parted from their bodies when they were buried. There seems to have been a roaring trade in Haydn skulls – with several doing the rounds in the years after his death. Many years later, the Australian composer and pianist Percy Grainger left instructions in his will, that his skeleton should be put on show at the University of Melbourne. The University turned down the generous offer on the grounds of public decency.

SYMPHONY

This is a large-scale piece, normally written for an orchestra. It usually has four separate movements, and was once considered the greatest challenge to which a composer could aspire. Like buses, they rarely come in ones. Having said that, unlike buses, they seem to come in nines – Beethoven, Schubert and Dvořák each wrote nine of them.

∽ TEN GREAT SYMPHONIES ∾
Beethoven: *No.9 (Choral)*
Mozart: *No.40*
Brahms: *No.2*
Dvořák: *No.9 (New World)*
Haydn: *No.94 (Surprise)*
Berlioz: *Symphonie Fantastique*
Mahler: *No.5*
Tchaikovsky: *No.5*
Shostakovich: *No.5*
Schubert: *No.8 (Unfinished)*

LUIGI BOCCHERINI (1743–1805)

Boccherini is best known for the *Minuet* from his *String Quintet No. 5*, which is just one of a total of 154 quintets he wrote for various different combinations of instruments. One out of 154. Life can be cruel, can't it?

All composers need to have financial backers to help them put food on the table while they're busy writing music. Boccherini relied heavily on Lucien Bonaparte. As well as being Napoleon's brother, he was also the French Ambassador to Spain. Despite Bonaparte's largesse, Boccherini was another of those composers who was stone cold broke when he died.

Check out: *Cello Concerto in G* (Boccherini himself was a bit of a whizz on the cello).

MRS HAYDN – THE TRUTH

Boccherini's musical style was, on occasions, somewhat reminiscent of that of the great Haydn. So, if you ever hear Boccherini referred to as 'the wife of Haydn', this is not a reference to an 18th century civil partnership, but rather the nickname he was given during his lifetime, because of the stylistic similarities of their music.

> *Since Mozart's day, composers have learnt the art of making music throatily and palpitatingly sexual.*
> **ALDOUS HUXLEY, WRITER**

BASSOON

The bassoon is the lowest woodwind instrument of the orchestra. It looks something like a didgeridoo wearing too much jewellery, but with an espresso frother coming out of the side. In fact, just like espresso, it too comes in single and double varieties.

Check out: Any of Vivaldi's 37 surviving bassoon concertos | Mozart: *Bassoon Concerto* | The theme from the children's television programme *Ivor the Engine*.

Name drop: Best not let on you know any bassoonists.

WOLFGANG AMADEUS MOZART (1756–1791)

You might know him as Wolfgang Amadeus Mozart – but his real name in full is Johannes Chrysostomus Wolfgangus Theophilus Mozart. 'Amadeus' is the Latin version of the Greek word 'Theophilus', which means 'loved by God'.

When those in the know sit down to debate 'Who's the greatest of them all?' Mozart and Beethoven usually end up coming first and second, although the top spot changes hands as often as a magician's playing card. Probably the best-known child prodigy, Mozart could play the keyboard by the age of three and could compose from five. He went on his first European tour when he was six and by the time he had reached the grand old age of twelve, he had finished two operas.

Mozart's dad, Leopold, loved to show off his son's talents as a way of making money. When the prodigy was just seven years old, his party trick was to cover the piano keyboard with a cloth and then to play fiendishly difficult pieces without being able to see any of the notes.

Mozart wrote four horn concertos during his relatively short life, so it's hard to believe that when he was a small boy, he was absolutely terrified of the instrument. One musician described how, when he blew his horn in

Wolfgang's direction, the colour instantly drained out of the boy's cheeks. The horn player seriously thought the young Mozart would have suffered a fit had he not stopped playing.

As an adult, Mozart could knock out a new piece of music in a matter of minutes. Once, when he was walking along the street, a beggar asked him for some money. Mozart was, as usual, a bit short of readies at the time, so he wrote out a tune on a piece of manuscript paper. He told the beggar to take it to a music publisher, who would exchange it for cash.

In the winter of 1781-1782, Mozart was challenged to a keyboard duel by the composer and piano-maker, Clementi. It was officially a tie, but while Clementi was graciously wowed by Mozart's abilities, Mozart's views on the event verge on the catty. He said that Clementi was 'mechanical' and played with 'no feeling'.

Mozart became a Freemason in December 1784. His lodge was called *Benificence,* but later merged with two other lodges to form *Newly-Crowned Hope.* Mozart was an active member, writing a lot of music for Masonic events, as well as the opera *The Magic Flute,* a Masonic allegory.

Mozart's music is an excellent choice if you're planning to go to a live classical concert for the first time. It's nice to know that he did have some faults though – he was said to be very arrogant, had a strange obsession with his rear end and was hopeless at managing his money. He was buried in an unmarked pauper's grave.

Check out: *Laudate Dominum* | *Requiem* | *Clarinet Concerto* | *Piano Concerto No. 21* | *Horn Concerto No. 4* | *Piano Concerto No. 24* | *Serenade No. 13 ('Eine kleine Nachtmusik')* | *Symphony No. 41 ('Jupiter')* | *Cosi fan tutte* | *Don Giovanni* | *The Magic Flute* | *The Marriage of Figaro* | The film *Amadeus.*

> *I write as a sow piddles.*
> **WOLFGANG AMADEUS MOZART, COMPOSER**

FAMOUS OPERAS: WHAT IS ACTUALLY GOING ON?

NO. 1: MOZART: *THE MAGIC FLUTE*
(OR *PAPAGENO WAS A ROLLING STONE*)

It is often said that *The Magic Flute* is Mozart's version of a panto – silly, camp in places and with a great stage baddie to boo and hiss (The Queen of the Night). The plot is bizarre, too, even by opera standards.

∞ THE PLOT ∞

Act 1

Prince Tamino is knocked unconscious by a monster, which is killed by three mysterious ladies, who quite fancy him. On waking, he meets a mischievous birdcatcher (is that really a job?) called Papageno. The Three Ladies (diddle-y-dit-di-dee) padlock Papageno's mouth for lying and show Tamino a picture of a beautiful girl, the daughter of the Queen. They tell him that she is a prisoner of nasty Zorastro and he decides he will free her. Scene change.

Pamina, the girl in the picture, is receiving the unwanted attentions of Zorastro's number two, Monastatos. Papageno sees him off, much to Pamina's delight. Scene change again.

Tamino tries to gain entry into three temples, but fails twice. At the third attempt, a speaker emerges and tells him that Zorastro is no baddie after all, but that the Queen of the Night *is*. Tamino sings and plays his magic flute (yes, THE magic flute) and soothes a few savage beasts in the process. He scarpers, stage right, though, when he hears Papageno's pan-pipe (NOT the magic flute). In true panto style, Papageno enters stage left, with Pamina. When Monastatos enters and things look like turning ugly, Papageno plays his magic chimes (there's a lot of it about – magic, that is) and Monastatos dances off. Zorastro now enters, amidst huge pomp. Pamina and Papageno explain what had been going on so, when Monastatos arrives, dragging our hero Tamino, he gets short shrift and is sent off, with his ear now home to a flea. Oh, and a good flogging. Well, this is before the corporal punishment ban. Zorastro also asks Papageno and Tamino to prove themselves. Exciting. End of Act 1. Time for a Chunky Choc Ice.

Act 2

Tamino and Papageno's ordeals kick off. They are left alone, but who should show up but the Three Ladies (diddle-y-dit-di-dee), who try to persuade them to give it all up and nip off for a cheeky cappuccino. Both stay shtumm, and, so, Zorastro appears to tell them they have passed test number one. Scene change.

Pamina is asleep. The sleazy Monastatos slimes up to her, intent on who knows what, but is forced back by the Queen of the Night – he must be getting used to this by now. The evil Queen slings Pam a dagger and asks her to kill Zorastro. Slimeball Monastatos slithers up to Pam, again, and says he'll tell all – about the dagger – to Zorastro, if she doesn't... you know! Zorastro arrives not a moment too soon and dispatches Monastatos – now with veritable colony of fleas in his aural canal. Scene change.

Papageno meets his future love, Papagena, who is, shall we say, mature in years and displeasing of fizzog. Papageno is not exactly impressed. Meanwhile, Pamina has hooked up with Tamino, but he's still on his sponsored silence and she's heartbroken that he won't speak to her. Zorastro appears to tell Pam and Tam to say what could be their final goodbye. Papageno is forced to swear undying love to the somewhat facially challenged crone. When he does – PUFF! – she's transformed into the young and beautiful Papagena, although they can't be together until Pap has proved himself.

Tamino is then led off for his final ordeals – fire and water. With Pamina in tow, he passes with flying colours, dropping only a few minor points for not using his mirror. Papageno is also cheered up when he is allowed to be with Papagena. Just to round things off, Zorastro vanquishes the Queen of the Night and her Three Ladies (diddle-y-dit-di-dee) in a huge flood of bright, do-gooding light. All are happy, the opera is over and it's time to join the mad rush to get your coat from the cloakroom.

The most expensive musical manuscript ever to be sold at auction was a collection of nine of Mozart's symphonies, which went under the hammer in 1987 for £2.58 million. Six years later, the second most expensive musical score was auctioned off. Its buyer paid £2.13 million for a 575 page manuscript of Beethoven's *Symphony No. 9*.

> *It is sobering to consider that when Mozart was my age, he had already been dead for a year.*
> **TOM LEHRER, SATIRIST**

Ethel played all the right notes, but not necessarily in the right order.

A BOX OF MOZART

Every year, thousands of people visit Salzburg and literally eat Mozart. Don't worry, cannibalism isn't rife in Austria – Mozart is a brand of chocolate over there. It particularly appeals to visiting tourists.

SYMPHONIC VARIATION

Mozart wrote 41 symphonies but you could go to Jupiter and back before you find his symphony number 37. It doesn't actually exist. The symphony that was erroneously labelled Mozart's symphony no. 37 was actually composed by someone else. Mozart had copied it out for his friend. Of course, if you ever see a manuscript of it in a junkshop, snap it up anyway!

EINE KLEINE COOL MUSIK

When Mozart came to London on tour, he stayed at 20 Frith Street, lodging with one Thomas Williamson. There's a plaque on the wall of the house and, today, fans of a different kind of music stand and stare at it – it's directly opposite Ronnie Scott's Jazz Club.

> *If I were a dictator, I should make it compulsory for every member of the population between the ages of four and eighty to listen to Mozart for at least a quarter of an hour daily for the coming five years.*
> **SIR THOMAS BEECHAM, CONDUCTOR**

HITTING THE HIGH NOTES

When you hear Mozart's beautiful soprano motet, *Exultate jubilate,* does it make your eyes water? It could be because it was originally written not for a soprano at all, but for the castrato Venanzio Rauzzini.

NOTE PERFECT

After he had heard a performance of Mozart's *The Abduction from the Seraglio* in 1782, Emperor Joseph II turned to the composer and said: 'Too fine for our ears, my dear Mozart, and far too many notes'. From the composer came the retort: 'Exactly as many notes as are necessary, your Majesty'.

WAS MOZART MURDERED?

Almost certainly not. However, the story did do the rounds that Antonio Salieri saw off his rival by poisoning him. This tale gained a modicum of credence because Mozart 'foresaw' his own death when a tall dark stranger came to his door and commissioned him to write his *Requiem.* Rather than being Salieri dressed up, or as Mozart believed, 'Death' himself (without the scythe), this was in fact the servant of a nobleman who wanted Mozart to write the work anonymously, before passing it off as his own. Poor old Mozart was by then seriously ill and the doorstep visitation contributed to a severe worsening of his state of mind and of his health in general.

CONCERTO

A piece of music, usually in three movements, written for a solo instrument accompanied by an orchestra. When a concerto is performed, the soloist, who is very much the star of the show, usually sits at the front of the stage next to the conductor. Incidentally, in music, a movement does not refer to the stampede towards the bar at the interval of a concert. Instead, it is one section of a bigger piece. Usually, different movements are played at different speeds, indicated by those Italian instructions of which composers are so fond.

∞ TEN GREAT CONCERTOS ∞
Rachmaniniov: *Piano Concerto No. 2*
Beethoven: *Piano Concerto No. 5 ('Emperor')*
Mozart: *Clarinet Concerto*
Bruch: *Violin Concerto No. 1*
Elgar: *Cello Concerto*
Grieg: *Piano Concerto*
Rodrigo: *Concierto De Aranjuez*
Shostakovich: *Piano Concerto No. 2*
Mendelssohn: *Violin Concerto*
J.S. Bach: *Double Violin Concerto*

LUDWIG VAN BEETHOVEN (1770–1827)

Along with Mozart, Beethoven has a strong claim on the title 'the world's greatest classical composer'. He wrote everything: concertos, an opera, choral works, pieces for solo instruments – you name it – but his speciality was the symphony. He led a tough life, often beaten, early on, by his alcoholic father. In his twenties, his doctor told him that he was going deaf and by the time he was in his thirties, he had totally lost his hearing.

The supreme quality of the works which he wrote and never actually heard remains one of the great marvels of classical music. By the time his magnificent *Symphony No. 9* received its premiere, he was completely deaf. For the first public performance, he sat on the stage with his back to the audience. At the end of the concert, it was only when one of the singers turned him around to face the crowd that he realised that they had been wildly cheering and applauding his masterpiece.

His best known work for solo piano, *The Moonlight Sonata*, wasn't given the name by Beethoven himself. It acquired the title from a critic, who thought that the piece evoked an image of the moon over Lake Lucerne.

Beethoven's *Symphony No. 3* was going to be dedicated to Napoleon Bonaparte. But when the composer heard that his hero had crowned himself 'Emperor', he ran to his manuscript and crossed out the dedication. In its place he put 'Eroica' – the hero – adding the words 'to the *memory* of a great man'.

Fellow composer Franz Schubert was one of the pall-bearers at Beethoven's funeral. In total, more than 30,000 people paid their respects at the service.

Check out: *Symphony No. 5,* which must have the most famous opening bars in all classical music | *Symphony No. 6 ('Pastoral')* | *Symphony No. 9 ('Choral')* – particularly the magnificent final movement, *The Ode to Joy.*

> *Last night the band played Beethoven.*
> *Beethoven lost.*
> **ANON**

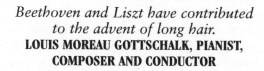

> *Beethoven and Liszt have contributed*
> *to the advent of long hair.*
> **LOUIS MOREAU GOTTSCHALK, PIANIST,**
> **COMPOSER AND CONDUCTOR**

After an eerie silence where his solo should have been,
it slowly dawned on the rest of the band that the trombonist had fallen
through a hole in the floor.

FAMOUS OPERAS: WHAT IS ACTUALLY GOING ON?

NO.2: BEETHOVEN: *FIDELIO* (OR *JAILHOUSE ROCCO*)

It has been said that Beethoven was not particularly a fan of opera, writing only this one. He did try to make up for this by writing far too many overtures for it though – four, in the end. Beethoven revised it quite a few times after the first version flopped, and it now stands at only two acts rather than the original three. He did think about venturing out on another opera, even writing the odd sketch for his own version of *Macbeth*. But in the end, this was to be his one and only.

It's all about Leonore, whose husband, Florestan, has disappeared. He worked for the State Department, and no one will believe Leonore when she says she smells a rat. She has narrowed her search to a jail near Seville. She gets a job in the prison, disguised as a man. You see? The opera's not even begun yet, and, already, it's a cock and bull story.

∞ THE PLOT ∞

Act 1

We're in a prison courtyard. Jaquino is the jailer's assistant and Marzelline is the jailer's daughter. Jaquino loves Marzelline, but – and this could be problematic – Marzelline loves the jailer's new assistant, Fidelio. Of course, as we know, Fidelio is a girl. Rocco, the jailer, comes in and they all sing in a quartet. Rocco then waxes lyrical on the subject of money, how lovely it is and how he'd like lots of it. Fidelio (or should we say Leonore) offers to do lots of his dirty work for him, and Rocco says how great he thinks he (she) is.

The prison governor, Pizzarro, arrives and tells Rocco that the Minister of State, Don Fernando, is coming to check up on the prison. Pizarro says that Rocco should do away with… you know who – Prisoner X! Rocco doesn't really want to. Pizarro says he'll do it himself. Fidelio (Leonore) hears all this and is more than a little incensed. She has big plans for a rescue attempt. She persuades Rocco to allow the prisoners out into the open air, because it's the King's birthday. She eagerly watches their faces to see if her husband, Florestan, is amongst them. He isn't. Fidelio (Leonore) then gathers that she has to help Rocco dig a grave in the dungeon cell. It could be her husband's cell. She could save him! Or if not, she could jump in the grave with him, and they could die together. This thought cheers her up no end. End of Act 1 – time for an expensive tin of travel sweets and a coffee with plastic pot of creamer.

Act 2

As the music descends, so do we... into the dungeon. Florestan is indeed there, in chains. He's a bit worse for wear, as you can imagine, and, apart from anything else, is seeing visions of his gorgeous Leonore. Rocco and Fidelio (Leonore) come down to his dungeon. Fidelio (Leonore) gives him a drink and a little bit of food. Naturally, he's quite grateful. Cue Pizarro, who pulls out his dagger and moves to kill Florestan. Fidelio (Leonore) rushes to stand between them, revealing herself as Leonore (not literally, of course). A fanfare above tells them that the Minister of State has arrived. Pizarro has missed his moment and the game is up. All the prisoners are freed, the Minister of State recognises Florestan and orders Leonore to set him free, and Pizarro is arrested. Large ones all round.

> **Having adapted Beethoven's sixth symphony for Fantasia, Walt Disney commented:** *'Gee! That'll make Beethoven'.* **MARSHALL MCLUHAN, MEDIA COMMENTATOR, *CULTURE IS OUR BUSINESS* (1970)**

DISC COUNT

It's claimed that compact discs hold 74 minutes of music to ensure that the whole of Beethoven's *Symphony No. 9* could be fitted on one disc without any interruptions.

> *You can chase a Beethoven symphony all your life and not catch up.* **ANDRÉ PREVIN, CONDUCTOR AND COMPOSER**

SONATA

A piece of music usually written either for a solo instrument, or for any single instrument with a piano. A sonata is written in three or four movements and follows a set of rules so complicated, it would make the Civil Service jealous.

☞ TEN GREAT SONATAS ☜
Beethoven: *Piano Sonata No. 8 (Pathétique)*
Beethoven: *Piano Sonata No. 14 (Moonlight)*
Beethoven: *Piano Sonata No. 23 (Appassionata)*
Beethoven: *Violin Sonata No. 9 (Kreutzer)*
Mozart: *Piano Sonata No. 11*
Tartini: *Violin Sonata in G minor (Devil's Trill)*
Chopin: *Piano Sonata No. 2*
Rachmaninov: *Piano Sonata No. 2*
Elgar: *Violin Sonata*
Mendelssohn: *Cello Sonata No. 1*

> *The notes I handle no better than many pianists. But the pauses between the notes – ah, that is where the art resides.*
> **ARTUR SCHNABEL, PIANIST**

TAKING IT ON THE CHIN

The German composer Louis Spohr was a revolutionary of sorts. As well as being one of the first conductors to use a baton to keep time, he also invented the chin rest for the violin, sometime around 1820.

NICCOLÒ PAGANINI (1782–1840)

As well as composing, Paganini was one of classical music's greatest showmen and is said to have been the fastest violinist ever. Officials once measured him doing twelve notes to the second. He encouraged the rumour that he had sold himself to the devil in exchange for his phenomenal fiddling fingers. One concert reviewer said he could see a small demon-like creature, perched on Paganini's shoulder, throughout a performance.

Check out: *Violin Concerto No. 1* | *Violin Concerto No.2.*

Name drop: Berlioz. Paganini commissioned the viola concerto *Harold in Italy* from Berlioz, but didn't like it when it arrived, so refused to pay or play. He later changed his mind, kneeling at Berlioz's feet and giving him a cheque for 20,000 francs.

> *Rossini would have been a great composer if his teacher had spanked him enough on the backside.*
> **LUDWIG VAN BEETHOVEN, COMPOSER**

GIOACHINO ROSSINI (1792–1868)

Another of the great Italian opera composers, Rossini was a one-man hit factory until he was 37. Then, suddenly, he stopped writing altogether and for the last thirty years of his life his only really major work was the choral piece *Stabat Mater*. Nobody is quite sure why. By then, though, he had racked up enormous success at home and abroad.

In 1816, when Rossini's opera *The Barber of Seville* – now one of the most performed operas in the world – was premiered, the audience booed and shouted the name 'Paisiello' over and over again. The reason? Paisiello had composed a version of the opera long before Rossini's and his was much more popular at the time. History changed all that though.

Rossini loved his food, so it seems appropriate that his name has been attached to more dishes than any other composer. As well as *Tournedos Rossini*, which is steak layered on croutons with foie gras and truffles on top, you will also find dishes such as *Omelette Rossini* and *Salade Rossini*.

Check out: *'Largo al factotum'* from *The Barber of Seville* | Overture to *The Silken Ladder* | Overture to *The Thieving Magpie* | Overture to *William Tell*.

Well, I Never! Rossini claimed to have written the whole of *The Barber of Seville* in just thirteen days.

Name drop: Isabella Colbran and Olympe Pélissier. Isabella was Rossini's soprano wife; Olympe was the mistress whom, when Isabella died, he married.

THE ORIGINAL KING OF RECYCLING

For Rossini, recycling was not about taking his empties to the bottle bank or bundling up old piles of paper. He was shameless about how he recycled his own music. The overture for his opera *Aureliano in Palmira* was used again as the overture for his subsequent opera *Elizabeth Queen of England,* and then he had no pangs of conscience about using it all over again as the overture to *The Barber of Seville.* This time, it became a smash hit and we normally think of it as being attached to this opera, rather than the other two, when we hear it today.

> *How wonderful the opera world would be if there were no singers.*
> **GIOACHINO ROSSINI, COMPOSER**

From the moment Gertrude began playing, the Reverend Smythe was bewitched by her amazing cadenzas.

FAMOUS OPERAS: WHAT IS ACTUALLY GOING ON?

NO. 3: ROSSINI: THE BARBER OF SEVILLE
(OR *SOMETHING FOR THE WEAK END*)

Rossini took a bit of risk setting his own version of the Barber of Seville story, mainly because there already existed a version by the composer Paisiello. Back then, Paisiello was far more popular than Rossini. The gamble paid off though. So much so that, today, Rossini's name is almost synonymous with opera, whereas Paisiello's is usually followed by the word 'who?'.

∞ THE PLOT ∞

Act 1

Dr Bartolo has a ward, the young and beautiful Rosina. Count Almaviva fancies Rosina, but Bartolo keeps a watchful eye on her. Almaviva gets his servant, Fiorello, to serenade her with musicians. Amidst the general cacophony of musicians, Figaro enters. Figaro is Dr Bartolo's barber. Of course he is. Who else would he be? He announces himself in one of the most famous arias ever (the 'Figaro, Figaro, Figaro, Figaro...' one).

Rosina has noticed Almaviva, though, and drops a letter from her balcony asking him his name. He tells her it is Lindoro. (Thus obeying opera rule number one – 'Never use your real name if a false one could be more confusing'). Meanwhile, as Dr Bartolo tells his singing teacher that he suspects Almaviva of being after his ward, Figaro manages to let Rosina know that his 'cousin Lindoro' (Almaviva, yes? Are you keeping up?) is crazy about her. Dr Bartolo lectures her on dropping letters from the balcony and about what will happen if she crosses him.

Meanwhile, Lindoro (the artist formerly known as Almaviva) gets into Rosina's house disguised as, wait for it... a tipsy soldier. What else? He then claims the right to be billeted there. Genius. He makes himself known to Rosina and refuses to take a blind bit of notice of Rosina's governess, the singing teacher, and even the police, who arrive in a scene more reminiscent of the great Keystone Cops than the great composers. General mayhem ensues. Interval. Time for a Cherry Brandy.

Act 2

Almaviva, aka Lindoro aka Tipsy Soldier, is now dressed up as Don Alonso, a new music teacher, supposedly sent by Bartolo's own music teacher, whom he says is ill. He tells Bartolo that he has a letter from Almaviva (himself) and says he will persuade Rosina that it was given to him by one of Almaviva's (that's himself) many mistresses, thus making Almaviva (himself, remember) look bad. Figaro then enters, wanting to shave Bartolo. Well, he is a barber. Bartolo says 'No', but Figaro insists, creates a bit of a diversion and manages to get Almaviva (aka Lindoro aka Tipsy Soldier aka Don Alonso) and Rosina together for a few moments. Cue the real music teacher, who is not ill. Almaviva (aka… etc) and Figaro persuade him that he IS ill, and should go home. Figaro then shaves Bartolo, while Almaviva and Rosina secretly – but not secretly enough – plan to run away together. We say 'not secretly enough' because, of course, Bartolo overhears them. When he has sent Almaviva packing, Bartolo shows Rosina the letter from Almaviva, telling her it's from one of his mistresses. Slightly annoyed, Rosina spills her guts to Bartolo about the planned elopement, and agrees to marry Bartolo.

But suddenly, out of nowhere, a storm blows up. Figaro and Almaviva show up and, of course, Al and Rosina make up. Figaro has planned their escape with a ladder to the balcony. When the ladder disappears, though, Figaro realises that they've been rumbled. But, as luck would have it, the *deus ex machina* turns up in the form of… a notary. Of course. Who else would show up just then but someone who is able to marry people? In fact, he was there to marry Bartolo and Rosina, but instead marries Almaviva and Rosina. In the end, everyone comes round to the idea – even Bartolo who is offered money by Almaviva as a compensation for Rosina's dowry. Love, or at least a mixture of love and money, changes everything.

> *Give me a laundry list and*
> *I will set it to music.*
> **GIOACHINO ROSSINI, COMPOSER**

10 CLASSICAL WORKS USED IN TV THEME TUNES

FRANZ SCHUBERT (1797–1828)

Some composers seem to find one thing and stick to it like glue. If Schubert is salt, then songs (or, as he would have said, 'Lieder') are pepper. Despite dying at the age of 31, he composed more than 600 of them. To be fair, he also found time for more or less nine symphonies (one was unfinished), eleven operas and around 400 other pieces. All of this was completed in a composing career that lasted for just 18 years. In 1815 alone, he wrote 140 songs, including eight in one day in October, along with a symphony, two masses and assorted other works. He also liked to have fun and in his day, he was famous for his musical parties known as *Schubertiads*.

Schubert stood at only 5'1" in his stockinged feet. This diminutive frame, added to his rather plump body, earned him the nickname 'Schwammerl' among his friends. This translates as 'the little mushroom'.

Check out: *Marche Militaire No. 1* | Overture and Incidental Music to *Rosamunde* | *Piano Quintet ('Trout')* based on one of his songs | *Piano Sonata No. 21* | *Symphony No. 8 ('Unfinished')*.

Well, I Never! Schubert was a notoriously bad timekeeper. His friends' letters are strewn with references to him being tardy or not showing up at all.

CHAMBER MUSIC

So called because it was written for groups small enough to play in the privacy of their own chamber, or room. Replaced nowadays by the Nintendo Wii. Chamber music can be for anything from a couple of soloists to larger chamber orchestras, which usually have up to 30 or so players. That's compared with a full symphony orchestra, which can have as many as 80 to 100 performers on the stage at any one time.

TEN GREAT CHAMBER WORKS
Mendelssohn: *Octet*
Schubert: *Piano Quintet ('Trout')*
Mozart: *Clarinet Quintet*
Schubert: *String Quintet D956*
Borodin: *String Quartet No. 2*
Schubert: *String Quartet No. 14 ('Death and the Maiden')*
Tchaikovsky: *String Quartet No. 1*
Beethoven: *Grosse Fuge*
Mozart: *Trio for Clarinet, Viola and Piano in E Flat ('Kegelstatt Trio')*
Saint-Saëns: *Carnival of the Animals* – although this work is most often performed by a full orchestra nowadays, it was originally written for two pianos, string quintet, flute, clarinet, glockenspiel, and xylophone. Admittedly, you would need a big front room to fit that lot in.

GAETANO DONIZETTI (1797–1848)

Along with his contemporaries Bellini and Rossini, Donizetti is thought of as being one of the greatest exponents of *bel canto* opera. Literally translated from the Italian as 'beautiful singing', this style developed in the 19th century. Donizetti's most enduring work is his 1835 opera *Lucia di Lammermoor,* which contains the smash hit aria '*Una furtiva lagrima*'. Donizetti died a sad death, in the grip of clinical insanity.

FAMOUS OPERAS: WHAT IS ACTUALLY GOING ON?

NO. 4: DONIZETTI: *THE ELIXIR OF LOVE* (OR *FINDING NEMORINO*)

Donizetti was 'Mr Opera' in the first half of the 19th century. He wrote his first opera at the age of 21 and then continued at a rate of just over three operas every year after that, until forced to stop by paralysis at the age of 48.

The Elixir of Love was written in less than two weeks, when the manager of the Teatro della Canobbiana in Milan begged Donizetti to help him out. The composer of his scheduled opera had let him down and he suggested that Donizetti might just nip and tuck an old one. Suitably challenged, Donizetti and his words man, Romani, set to work and produced one of his most loved operas in a fortnight. If this was Wagner, that would be the length of the opera.

∽ THE PLOT ∾

Act 1
First, let's set the scene: we're in the countryside. Adina is the love interest in this opera and we're outside her farm. Nemorino, a village peasant, is sitting watching her read, all the while bemoaning the fact that she could never love a lowly idiot like him. Adina looks up from her book and laughs. She tells her friends she's reading the story of Tristan and Isolde, and says that Tristan won his love by giving her a magic love potion, which meant she couldn't keep her hands off him. Nemorino likes the sound of this potion. Some soldiers enter. The sergeant, Belcore, gives Adina a bunch of flowers and asks her to marry him. Adina is chuffed but turns him down. Nemorino, still looking on (these days it would be called stalking) wishes he had Belcore's courage to just go up to someone and propose.

When they are alone, Nemorino tries to pour out his feelings. Adina says she is just too flighty to be any use to him. In the village square, a travelling salesman has arrived. He's one of those quack doctors offering slightly dodgy cures for everything. Nemorino asks him for Isolde's Love Potion, please. The Doctor, who's called Dulcamara, sees him coming. Dulcamara sells Nemorino a flask of wine, telling him it's a brilliant love potion that will work by the next day. Nemorino downs the whole 'potion' and is soon steaming drunk. As a result, not only is he loud and laddish, he's also not particularly bothered about Adina. His couldn't-care-less attitude annoys her because she's not used to being ignored. When Belcore comes in, she agrees to marry him. And within six days, too (he's being posted somewhere else and wants to wed before he goes). Still miffed that Nemorino is ignoring her, she even agrees to marry Belcore today. Nemorino is gobsmacked and begs her just to wait one day, thinking his 'potion' will kick in. Belcore tells him to lay off and then he and Adina head off to see the notary. How depressed is Nemorino? He decides he needs some expert help – Dr Dulcamara! End of Act 1, time for warm Kia-Ora and popcorn.

Act 2

Adina and Belcore's wedding banquet – but, don't worry, they haven't signed on the dotted line yet. They've just decided to get on with the party until the notary arrives. The bride and groom-to-be sing songs to each other. Meanwhile, Nemorino asks Dulcamara to help him, and is told that only more elixir can do the trick. But Nemorino is completely broke. Belcore then persuades Nemorino that, if he signs up to the army, he'll get twenty scudi. Nemorino signs the forms and runs off to find Dulcamara.

While he's away, news arrives that Nemorino's uncle has died, leaving him all his money. Although he doesn't know it, Nemorino is now a bit of a hot property, top of the list of eligible bachelors. As a result, when Nemorino returns, with yet more wine/potion down him, the girls flock round him like flies. Of course, he thinks it's the potion. Adina walks in and is more than a little miffed to find everyone suddenly loves Nemorino. She also tries to tell him that he shouldn't have joined the army, but he is dragged off by one of a bunch of eager women suitors. Dulcamara explains to Adina that he sold him a 'potion' – and offers to sell her one. It is at this point that Nemorino returns and sees Adina, with a tear in her eye. He realises that she must love him, after all. (The aria that goes with this, *'Una Furtiva Lagrima'*, is one of the most beautiful tenor arias ever). Adina buys Nemorino out of the army, and then admits to him that she loves him. Belcore is only slightly miffed, showing what sort he was all along. Dulcamara tries to claim that, as Nemorino is now rich, he can add 'wealth' to the long list of benefits of his love potion. All his wine/potion sells like hot cakes and he rides off into the sunset.

> *Every composer knows the anguish*
> *and despair occasioned by forgetting ideas*
> *which one has no time to write down.*
> **HECTOR BERLIOZ, COMPOSER**

HECTOR BERLIOZ (1803–1869)

If you are looking for a 'patron saint of the Romantic period', then you could do worse than alight upon floppy-fringed Frenchman, Hector Berlioz. Hector was a bit of a luvvie, and, indeed, Hector's house was often home to some rather wild, over-dramatic behaviour. He once pursued an ex-lover with pistols and poison. Another he followed disguised as a maid. Say no more.

Check out: *Symphonie Fantastique* | the oratorio *The Childhood of Christ* | His *Requiem*, which was written for a HUGE chorus and orchestra as well as four brass bands – one at each corner of the stage.

Name drop: Harriet Smithson, the Irish actress Berlioz was nuts about. He wooed her, won her and wed her. Of course, then he got bored of her and started craving other women. An artist's life, eh?

> On Hector Berlioz's *Symphonie Fantastique*:
> *What a good thing this isn't music.*
> **GIOACHINO ROSSINI, COMPOSER**

> Also about Hector Berlioz:
> *One ought to wash one's hands after dealing with one of his scores.*
> **FELIX MENDELSSOHN, COMPOSER**

> Mendelssohn on Berlioz again:
> *A regular freak, without a vestige of talent.*

SAXOPHONE

As musical instruments go, the saxophone is one of the new kids on the block. It was invented by a Belgian called Adolphe Sax around 1840. Even though saxophones are made of brass, they sit in the woodwind section of the orchestra because they're similar to play to the clarinet. Without a doubt, they occupy a special position as the coolest of the wind instruments.

Check out: Debussy, Vaughan Williams, Berlioz, Bizet and Glazunov have all written pieces featuring the sax. Their popularity has been somewhat overshadowed recently by *'Parce Mihi Domine'* from the album *Officium,* a collaboration between the jazz saxophonist Jan Garbarek and the early music vocal group, the Hilliard Ensemble. The sound that they create is crossover music at its very best.

Name drop: British sax player John Harle | The teenage saxophone sensation, Tyler Rix, who became famous following his success on the *Classical Star* reality television programme.

$\oint$

ADOLPHE ADAM (1803–1856)

This French composer of opera and ballet is best known today for his Christmas carol *O Holy Night*, which has been sung by a host of different stars and has been voted at or near the top of the list of the nation's favourite carols by Classic FM listeners in the station's annual festive poll (See page 162). It's also said to have been the first piece of music ever broadcast on the radio. Adam was regarded as an excellent teacher during his lifetime and he counted Delibes among his pupils. When he got into financial difficulties after investing his own money in a new Parisian opera house, he turned to music criticism and journalism to help pay the bills.

Check out: Adam's ballet *Giselle*.

FAMOUS BALLETS: WHAT IS ACTUALLY GOING ON?

NO. 1: ADAM: *GISELLE*
(OR... *'YOUR DANCING'S GIVING ME THE WILLIES'*)

Giselle has a score composed by Adolphe Adam and original choreography by Jean Coralli, a massive choreographer in his day, with help from dancer Jules Perrot, a man described as having 'the perfect legs of a Greek statue'. The ballet was a huge hit for Adam and his team, and it instantly travelled round the world, with productions in London, St. Petersburg, Milan, Vienna, and even as far afield as Boston. Later, it was revived by legendary choreographer Petipa, for the Russian Imperial Ballet, and his steps are usually the ones seen today.

Act 1

There's a Count, called Albrecht. One day, possibly after having read *The Prince and the Pauper*, he decides to dress up as a peasant and wander into the nearest village. Deep in Pleb Central, he encounters the young Giselle. Giselle is perfect in every way, if a little bit prone to romantic histrionics, which verge on complete and utter madness. One look at the Count, and, that's it – she's gone. Out for the count, you might say. At this point, the bizarrely named Hilarion enters. He's the local 'bloke' and, to be fair, had his eye on Giselle long before Albrecht was on the scene. Hilarion warns Giselle that her new love will end in tears. She doesn't listen. (Why would you listen to someone called Hilarion?) Instead, she dances a love duet with Albrecht.

Suddenly, a hunting party is heard. The Count decides he should hide, as the party might include Bathilde, his fiancée. Yes, that's the fiancée he had carelessly forgotten to mention to Giselle. As you'd expect, it is indeed Bathilde coming round the corner. Naturally, Bathilde entrances the entire party with her riches, giving Giselle a green necklace. Giselle is over the moon. She may have no money, no food, no hope *and* be dining in the Last Drop of Sanity saloon, but at least she has a green necklace. Wonderful. The hunting party leaves and Albrecht reappears, as does Hilarion. Hilarion accuses Albrecht of being a bounder. Giselle defends him, until the hunting party suddenly returns. Bathilde lovingly greets her fiancée, Albrecht, at which point Giselle immediately trips off to La La Land – first class, one way. No sooner does she arrive, though, than she dies of shock – the shock of a betrayed love.

Curtain closes. Morbid faces all around in the stalls circle bar. Some folk are throwing themselves off the amphitheatre. And it's still only the end of the first act.

Act 2

We're in a forest. It's night time. Hilarion, whose name now seems like a very bad joke indeed, is looking for the grave of Giselle. She has been buried in the forest. Nice. Suddenly, a crowd of spirits show up. These are called The Willies – honestly. They are the ghosts of all the women who have been jilted so, as you can imagine, not the friendliest bunch in the world. They have the habit of engaging any man passing their way in a ghoulish dance of death – and, of course, being already dead themselves, it's the passing man who gets the death bit. They summon up the ghost of Giselle, who, having only just pegged it, is not yet a fully qualified Willi, rather more like an apprentice.

At this point, the Count enters. Dead Giselle, the trainee Willi, greets him. He is a little surprised to see her and even more surprised to see through her. He apologises. She accepts his apology. They dance. Of course they do. Just at this point, the Willies start to come back on. The Count and Dead Giselle exit, stage left, pursued by bare ladies, who are actually chasing Hilarion. Quite what this guy ever did to deserve this level of attention is never quite clear. Still, the Willies are taking no prisoners and they duly dance him to death. (His, not theirs). Soon, he is dancing with the fishes, although this particular *pas de beaucoup* is not choreographed.

At this point, the Willies go for Albrecht. 'About time!' you may well cry. They start to 'dance' him – note the transitive use of the verb – whereupon he begs for forgiveness. The Queen of the Willies, who is called Myrthe, (explains a little why they went after Hilarion), refuses to listen. Giselle interjects, and does a little dancing on Albrecht's behalf, so he can have a rest.

So, the ballet closes, with Albrecht rescued, Giselle dancing the dance of death herself, and thus, *not* forced to become a Willi for the rest of her death. She is laid to rest. Everyone leaves the theatre in stunned silence except small children who are crying their eyes out. Front of house staff try to hide anything sharp.

The ballet in brief: *Saturday Night Fever* meets *One Flew Over the Cuckoo's Nest*, with a hint of Demi Moore in *Ghost*.

Moral of the story: Don't count your blessings and *definitely* don't bless your Counts. And… go easy on the spirits; they're not good for you.

This is one of the great dynasties of classical music, something along the lines of what Kirk and Michael Douglas are to acting today. Johann Strauss Senior was born in 1804 and his son, Johann Strauss Junior, came into the world 19 years later. Johann Sr is known as the 'Father of the Waltz', having written 152 of them. Having said that, his most famous work is the infectiously-fun *Radetzky March,* which isn't actually a waltz at all. He also had the top orchestra in Vienna. That was, until his son Johann Jr came along. He was the Bill Gates of classical music, turning music for dancing into big business and giving us a whole host of waltzes in the process, including the most popular of them all, *By the Beautiful Blue Danube.* He had six orchestras running simultaneously and wrote nearly 400 waltzes during his life. His brothers Josef and Eduard (each of whom had around 300 compositions to their names) both ended up conducting one or other of Johann Jr's orchestras.

Check out: *Die Fledermaus* (The Bat), an operetta jam-packed with great tunes, and written when Johann Jr was 51.

> *Joking apart, Prince Albert asked me to go to him on Saturday at two o'clock so that I might try his organ before I leave England.*
> **FELIX MENDELSSOHN, COMPOSER**

FELIX MENDELSSOHN (1809–1847)

This German-born composer was a frighteningly clever child, excelling as a painter, poet, athlete, linguist and musician. He made his public debut as a pianist at the age of nine and by the time he was sixteen he had composed his *Octet for Strings*.

When he was 17, Mendelssohn composed the overture to Shakespeare's play *A Midsummer Night's Dream*. It took him another 17 years to get around to composing the rest of the incidental music to the play. Many brides and bridegrooms will be thankful that he did – the music he wrote includes the ubiquitous *Wedding March*, heard at marriage services up and down the country every week.

A tour of Scotland in 1829 resulted in the hugely popular *Hebrides Overture*. His music tends to be bright and cheerful – indeed his name, Felix, means happy in Latin - but he died at a tragically young age, only 38, having never really recovered from the death of his much-loved sister, Fanny, who was also a gifted musician.

Check out: O *for the wings of a dove* | *Songs without Words* | *Symphony No. 4 ('Italian')* | *Violin Concerto*.

Well, I Never! Just like Beethoven's *Moonlight Sonata*, all but a handful of Mendelssohn's *Songs without Words* have a title made up by a publisher. So, *Restlessness*, *The Fleecy Clouds*, *The Shepherd's Complaint* (for which he no doubt had an ointment) are all the work of a publisher's imagination.

He composes by splashing ink over his manuscript paper; the result is as chance wills it.
HECTOR BERLIOZ ON FELLOW COMPOSER, FRÉDÉRIC CHOPIN

FRÉDÉRIC CHOPIN (1810–1849)

Chopin was sort of the Henry Ford of composers, whose catchphrase might have been 'you can have any instrument as long as it's the piano'. Some would say he was a little obsessive about tinkling the ivories, writing no fewer than 169 different pieces for solo piano. And now for some trivia. His *Second Piano Concerto* was actually written before his *First Piano Concerto*. But his *First Piano Concerto* was published first, so even though the *Second Piano Concerto* was in fact written first, it has always been referred to as the second. This seemed to happen quite a lot with composers (see Bruckner, later).

Check out: *Nocturne Opus 9 No. 2* | *Prelude No. 15 ('The Raindrop')* | *Waltz No. 6 ('The Minute Waltz'* – which, in fact, usually takes about a minute-and-a-half to play because 'minute' in this case means 'tiny').

Name drop: George Sand, the pseudonym of the female novelist with whom Chopin had a long and stormy affair.

After playing Chopin, I feel as if I had been weeping over sins that I had never committed.
OSCAR WILDE, WRITER

I LEFT MY HEART IN... WARSAW

When Chopin died, he was buried in France. But before his body was placed in its coffin, his heart was removed and pickled in alcohol. In accordance with his final wishes, it was then taken to Poland. Except for a short period during the Second World War, when it was removed for safe-keeping, it has remained in a church there ever since.

POLE APART

The celebrated international concert pianist Ignacy Jan Padereweski became the Prime Minister of Poland in 1919. During his time in charge, he was one of the international statesmen who negotiated the Treaty of Versailles. Once he'd sorted out things on the diplomacy front, he resigned as prime minister and went back to tinkling the ivories on a full-time basis.

PIANO

Invented in Florence, around 1709, modern-day pianos come in many shapes and sizes. 'Piano' is short for 'pianoforte', which is the Italian for 'quiet loud'. It is so called because it was the first keyboard to possess dynamic range. The previous keyboard of choice – the harpsichord – could play at one volume only. The piano is also one of the few instruments that can play lots of notes at once – so virtually every composer wrote some great stuff for the piano.

Name drop: Lang Lang I Evgeny Kissin I Martha Argerich I Maria João Pires I Freddy Kempf I Jean-Yves Thibaudet I Alfred Brendel I Leif Ove Andsnes.

⌒ TEN GREAT PIANO WORKS ⌒
Rachmaninov: *Piano Concerto No. 2*
Beethoven: *Piano Concerto No. 5 ('Emperor')*
Grieg: *Piano Concerto*
Shostakovich: *Piano Concerto No. 2*
Beethoven: *Piano Sonata No. 14 ('Moonlight')*
Rachmaninov: *Piano Concerto No. 3*
Tchaikovsky: *Piano Concerto No. 1*
Mozart: *Piano Concerto No. 21*
Chopin: *Piano Concerto No. 1*
Schubert: *Piano Quintet ('Trout')*

DON'T JUDGE A BOOK BY ITS COVER

The Austrian pianist, composer and teacher, Carl Czerny, is seen today as having been something of an expert on the art of the piano, writing many books on the subject. However worthwhile the text on the inside of the book, he didn't seem to have the knack for coming up with that pithy best-selling title to go on the front cover. His book *Letters to a Young Lady on the Art of Playing the Pianoforte from the Earliest Rudiments to the Highest State of Cultivation* is a particular favourite.

NOCTURNE

Written for the piano, these short pieces were invented by the Irish composer John Field. Chopin then developed the idea further. They are perfect to listen to as a late evening wind-down, as they are intended to suggest the calm of the night.

Check out: Chopin: *Nocturne in A Flat* and Debussy: *Nocturnes for Orchestra*, decidedly different, yet equally rewarding, pieces.

HUMMING ALONG

The Canadian pianist Glenn Gould was one of classical music's great eccentric geniuses. He always hummed throughout his recordings, which is either rather charming or intensely irritating, depending on your point of view. Watching him perform must have been a bizarre experience, as he insisted on sitting on a chair that was just fourteen inches high, which meant that his eyes were at the same level as the keyboard. This chair was made for him by his father and he continued to use it even when it was worn through. He always kept a glass of distilled water on the floor nearby, while the piano itself always had to be placed on a rug. He absolutely hated personal contact and refused to shake hands with anyone, including the conductors on stage at his performances. Gould even went as far as creating pseudonyms, which allowed him to publish scathing reviews of his own works. Among the best-known of these were the German musicologist 'Karlheinz Klopwisser', the English conductor 'Sir Nigel Twitt-Thornwaite' and a New York cabbie, turned music reviewer, 'Theodore Slutz'.

> *In order to compose, all you have to do is remember a tune that nobody else thought of.*
> **ROBERT SCHUMANN, COMPOSER**

ROBERT SCHUMANN (1810–1856)

Schumann was a great composer, but as a performer he lived in the shadow of his wife Clara, a renowned concert pianist. He suffered from syphilis and depression, and attempted suicide by throwing himself into the Rhine at the age of 44. Two years later, he died in an asylum.

Check out: *Scenes from Childhood No. 7 – Dreaming* | *Fantasie in C* | *Piano Concerto* | The song cycle *Dichterliebe*.

FRANZ LISZT (1811–1886)

One of the great pianists of his time, a performance by Liszt was greeted by the sort of response that we would associate with a chart-topping pop superstar today. He enjoyed the rock 'n' roll lifestyle a good century before it had been invented and had a long list of sexual conquests – even after he took holy orders.

Liszt had a penchant for huge, flashy versions of other people's pieces. Like olives, they are an acquired taste.

Check out: *Hungarian Rhapsody No. 2* | *Liebestraum No. 3* | *Piano Sonata* | *Rhapsodie Espagnole.*

Well, I Never! When you go to see a piano concerto in concert, the position of the piano in relation to the orchestra is all down to Liszt. Up until he performed, the pianist used to face the audience. As the first real megastar of the piano, the heartthrob pianist decided he wanted to be seen by his fans so had the piano moved side on – and it stuck.

Albert kept back a little of last night's Chinese takeaway for a quiet moment during the Beethoven symphony.

GIUSEPPE VERDI (1813–1901)

The fact that when we think of Italy, we think of opera is in no small part down to this mischievous-looking man, considered by many to be the greatest of all Italian opera composers. Big tuneful hits fill his 26 operas and the majority of them remain on the bill of fare at opera houses around the world today. When *Aida* received its premiere in Italy, the audience loved it so much that the standing ovation lasted for no fewer than 32 curtain calls. Another of his other major works, the *Requiem*, is regarded as one of the greatest pieces of choral music ever written.

Check out: *'Celeste Aida'* and *The Grand March* from *Aida* | Overture to *La Forza Del Destino* | *'Questa o quella'* and *'La donna e mobile'* from *Rigoletto* | *'Sempre libera'* from *La Traviata* | *Anvil Chorus* from *Il Trovatore* | *Chorus of the Hebrew Slaves* from *Nabucco* | *'Dies Irae'* from the *Requiem*.

Well, I Never! 'Viva Verdi' was the most fashionable line of graffiti in the 1860s, found chalked on many an Italian wall. Italian nationalists were campaigning for the king, Victor Emmanuel, and the line stood for 'Viva Victor Emmanuel, Re D'Italia' – Long Live Victor Emmanuel, King of Italy. Great free publicity.

> A review of Verdi's opera *Rigoletto*,
> shortly after its premiere:
> Rigoletto *lacks melody. This opera*
> *has hardly any chance of being kept in*
> *the repertoire.*
> **GAZETTE MUSICALE DE PARIS**

NO. 5: VERDI: *LA TRAVIATA* (OR TB OR NOT TB)

Verdi got the plot of his opera from a play written by Alexandre Dumas, fils, the son of the guy who wrote *The Three Musketeers*. It's a great love story, set in Paris, with the only real baddie being tuberculosis.

∞ THE PLOT ∞

Act 1

There's a party going on, thrown by our heroine, Violetta, a good time girl of the Paris party scene, who is, by the time we meet her, already ill. Her friend, Gastone, tells her that 'my mate fancies you' – his mate being Alfredo. Alfredo then leads the assembled partygoers in a great drinking song after which he stays to talk to Violetta. He tells her he loves her and she, more or less, tells him she loves him. When everybody else has left, though, Violetta sings to herself about her new love, while at the same time telling herself to deny it. Short act, Act one. Barely time for a quick Oyster Shell.

Act 2

Time has clearly passed. Violetta and Alfredo are living together (in sin) in the country. All is well, apart from the fact that Alfie finds out that Vi has been selling her jewellery to meet the bills. Just as she receives a party invite to Paris, he decides to go off to the capital to raise money.

A guest is announced. It is Alfredo's father, Georgio. He asks her to give his son up, so that no whiff of scandal can attach itself to his family, especially as he's got his daughter's wedding coming up. As the two discuss the affair, each gradually grows on the other – the father sees her as not a gold-digger after all, and she sees his point so much that she agrees to give up her love. She writes Alfie a note, but he enters, so she hides it. She says goodbye. After she's gone, he is handed her letter – which says 'I've gone back to my old life, to be a kept woman of Baron Douphol's' – and, despite a word from his Dad, he rushes off to Paris. Scene change.

At the party of Violetta's friend Flora, Alfredo enters and, not far behind him, Baron Douphol, with Violetta on his arm. Alfredo insults Violetta in front of everyone, the Baron challenges him and Violetta faints. Dramatic stuff. When she recovers, she sings of her love for Alfredo. End of Act 2. Time for a Vanilla tub with its own spoon in the lid.

Act 3

Time has clearly passed, again. Violetta is on her deathbed. She wakes from her stupor to re-read a letter from Alfredo's Dad, telling her that the Baron was wounded in the duel and, more importantly, that Alfredo knows that she was forced to give him up. Oh, and P.S. he's on his way to see her. She talks of death, just before Alfie enters. He tells her he'll take her off to Paris and all will be ok. She'd love to believe him but, as Alfie looks on, she dies. Very sad. Cue the Kleenex.

MUSICAL CATALOGUERS

There's only one way to have your name attached to a masterpiece and that's to write one. Isn't it? Well, it is unless you happen to be one of the people who catalogue composers' works. Among them are:

Otto Erich Deutsch – Schubert – (D. numbers)
Anthony van Hoboken – Haydn – (Hob. Numbers)
Ralph Kirkpatrick – Scarlatti – (K. numbers)
Ludwig von Köchel – Mozart – (K. numbers)
Peter Ryom – Vivaldi – (RV. numbers)

RICHARD WAGNER (1813–1883)

Think Wagner, think 'extreme'. His music is extreme, and it tends to elicit extreme reactions from listeners. It's love or hate with him. People rarely use the word 'quite' in connection with Wagner. Despite his genius, he was a deeply flawed and unpleasant character – racist, anti-Semitic, Machiavellian and a serial philanderer with a monstrous ego. Without doubt an awful man. Nevertheless, the music he wrote was his one redeeming feature and you should try it before you completely make up your mind about him. His greatest achievement is the four operas that make up *The Ring Cycle,* which together last for more than 15 hours. No, that's not a misprint.

One of the stranger uses of Wagner's music came in the cartoon *What's Opera, Doc?* Bugs Bunny and his lifelong adversary Elmer Fudd can be heard singing along to parts of *The Valkyrie* and *Tannhäuser,* giving many youngsters their first taste of opera.

Check out: Overture to *The Flying Dutchman* | Prelude to Act 1 of *Lohengrin* | *Bridal Chorus* from *Lohengrin* | *Ride of the Valkyries* from *The Valkyrie,* which was used as American helicopters swooped into Vietnam in the film *Apocalypse Now* | *Siegfried's Funeral March* from *Götterdämmerung* | *Pilgrims' Chorus* from *Tannhäuser* | Prelude to *Tristan and Isolde.*

Name drop: the *Siegfried Idyll,* possibly the most special birthday present ever. Wagner wrote it for his new wife, Cosima. He smuggled a chamber orchestra of musicians onto the landing outside her bedroom in 1870 and had them play this new work for her. Definitely one better than breakfast in bed.

WAGNER QUOTES

Imagine this: all the composers have met up in the afterlife and a roll-call is being taken of their names. When it comes to Wagner, it turns out that he's the only one who's insisted on a separate room. He merits his own section not because we think he is the greatest, but because whenever musicians were looking for a target, more of them set their sights on Wagner than any other.

Wagner has lovely moments but awful quarters of an hour.
GIOACHINO ROSSINI, COMPOSER

I love Wagner, but music I prefer is that of a cat hung up by its tail outside a window and trying to stick to the panes of glass with its claws.
CHARLES BAUDELAIRE, POET

I like Wagner's music better than any other music. It is so loud that one can talk the whole time without people hearing what one says. That is a great advantage.
OSCAR WILDE, *THE PICTURE OF DORIAN GRAY* (1891)

One can't judge Wagner's opera Lohengrin *after a first hearing, and I certainly don't intend hearing it a second time.*
GIOACHINO ROSSINI, COMPOSER

About Wagner's opera *Parsifal*:
The kind of opera that starts at six o'clock and after it has been going three hours you look at your watch and it says 6:20.
DAVID RANDOLPH, CONDUCTOR

I can't listen to too much Wagner. I start to get the urge to conquer Poland.
WOODY ALLEN, *MANHATTAN MURDER MYSTERY* (1993)

I've been told that Wagner's music is better than it sounds.
MARK TWAIN, WRITER

FAMOUS OPERAS: WHAT IS ACTUALLY GOING ON?

NO. 6: WAGNER: *TRISTAN AND ISOLDE* (OR *I'D LIKE TO KNOW WHERE YOU GOT THE POTION*)

This is one of the shorter Wagner operas, weighing in at just a little over three and a half hours, as opposed to, say, the Ring Cycle of operas, which can take half a lifetime to perform. Indeed, several people have been 'lost' inside a Ring cycle, having entered but never made it out, never to be seen again. Police say there is very little they can do other than to keep an open mind.

∞ THE PLOT ∞

Act 1

Tristan is on his way back from Ireland to Cornwall. We know, we know – not the classic romantic setting one thinks of for an opera, but bear with us. With him, he had Isolde, whom he loves. Despite that, he is taking her back to marry his Uncle Mark, the King of Cornwall. When Isolde finds out that she is intended for Mark and not Tristan, she gets more than a little annoyed, invoking the elements to come to destroy the ship and all who sail in it. Isolde sends for Tristan and asks her lady in waiting to make up a death potion that she will give him to drink. Tristan arrives and Isolde proposes a toast 'to us!' Tristan drinks it, but, unknown to Isolde, her lady-in-waiting has substituted a love potion for the death potion. They sink into each others' arms. People crowd the deck and, amidst general jubilation, the lady-in-waiting tells them to get a room. Oh, but what will they tell King Mark? End of Act 1. Time for a Strawberry Mivvy.

Act 2

Everyone's gone out to hunt with King Mark, Tristan included. Isolde signals Tristan to come to her by putting out a lighted torch. Tristan arrives and they rush into each other's arms. They bed down for a night of lurve, hoping the dawn will never come. Despite warnings from the lady-in-waiting that the night will soon be over, they carry on loving, singing their song of yearning for death through love – the *Liebestod*. Dawn arrives and with it the King's party. The King is philosophical, if livid. The knight Melot wounds Tristan in the ensuing kerfuffle. End of Act 2. Time for a Mint Feast in the bar.

Act 3

Tristan is at his castle in Brittany – again, not the most romantic of settings, but still. He is wounded and lapsing in and out of consciousness. A shepherd is piping, keeping watch for the ship that will bring Isolde to heal his wounds. Tristan drifts through memories of Isolde, and how she healed his wounds before, back in Ireland. Suddenly, the piper pipes a jollier, sort of 'I-can-see-Isolde's-ship' type tune, and Tristan struggles to get up. In his eagerness, he tears the bandages from his wounds, and, when Isolde rushes in, he can only whisper her name before dying in her arms. Another ship docks – bearing King Mark et al. Tristan's faithful friend, Kurwenal, thinks they've come after Isolde and so goes for them, killing Melot, the guy who wounded Tristan. The lady-in-waiting, though, rushes in to say that she had confessed to the king about switching the death potion with the love potion, but Isolde doesn't care. She sings her Liebestod, and, staring at the body of her lover, falls upon him, dead. Strong stuff. You may need a small sharpener yourself.

CHARLES GOUNOD (1818–1893)

Gounod was writing music in Paris at the time when it was a seething hotbed of great romantic composers. His contemporaries include Chopin, Liszt and Berlioz. His most famous work is the opera *Faust*, which spawned the *Jewel Song* and *The Soldiers' Chorus*. But Classic FM listeners' favourite Gounod piece has proved to be *Judex* from his little-known oratorio, Mors et Vita.

Check out: *Ave Maria* (Gounod borrowed Bach's *Prelude No. 1* and put a second tune over the top of it).

Name drop: Alfred Hitchcock. Gounod's *Funeral March of a Marionette* was used as the theme to the TV series *Alfred Hitchcock presents…*

71

JACQUES OFFENBACH (1819–1880)

This is the man who let loose the *Can-Can* on an unsuspecting public back in 1858. It comes from the operetta *Orpheus in the Underworld,* which scandalised the chattering classes of Paris at the time of its premiere. Offenbach is also known for the *Barcarolle* from his opera *The Tales of Hoffmann.* There used to be a strange association of bad luck attached to his name, a bit like Macbeth in the theatre, whereby people would have to cross themselves if he was mentioned. Staying with the name theme, Offenbach was born in the town of Cologne and sometimes he would sign himself as 'O. de Cologne'. Offenbach was shunned by the Paris Opera-Comique, who refused to perform his works. So he set up his own theatre, the Bouffes-Parisiens and, instantly, his music took off. Within months, he had to move to bigger premises to accommodate the huge audiences.

Well, I Never! Offenbach once beat Johann Strauss Jr in a waltz-writing competition held by a French music publishing company.

> Obituary of Jacques Offenbach, the man who composed the *Can-Can*:
> *He has written nothing that will live, nothing that will make the world better. His name as well as his music will soon be forgotten.*
> **CHICAGO TRIBUNE**

TRICK QUESTION

You know those silly questions: 'Who wrote Beethoven's Fifth?' Or 'Which country's official song is the French National Anthem?' Well, just be careful if someone asks you 'Who wrote the overture to Offenbach's *Orpheus in the Underworld*?' Because it was actually added later by Carl Binder.

SOUNDS FAMILIAR

Classical composers aren't averse to reusing a story that someone else has told before. Take the mythological tale of Orpheus, for instance. Monteverdi used it for his opera *L'Orfeo* in 1607. Gluck wrote a new version in Italian in 1762 and in French in 1774. Then Offenbach told the story all over again in 1858 in his opera *Orpheus in the Underworld*.

CÉSAR FRANCK (1822–1890)

Here is one of those rarest of beasts – a famous Belgian. And unlike Hercule Poirot or Tintin, César Franck actually existed. He never really had much success with his music during his life. In fact, the first glimmer of critical approval only came in the weeks before he died.

Check out: *Panis Angelicus* – a wedding classic | *Symphonic Variations for Piano and Orchestra.*

ANTON BRUCKNER (1824–1896)

Anton Bruckner was a simple man, wracked with self-doubt. So much so that he abandoned working on his First Symphony, thinking it not good enough. He started on his second, which he called his first symphony. When he later went back to complete his original symphony, he called it *Die Nulte* which translates as something like *The Nothing*[th] or *The Zero*[th].

Check out: *Symphony No. 7* | *Symphony No. 8.*

Well, I Never! If you ever go to the monastery of St. Florian in Vienna, have a look at the organ. Bruckner is buried under it.

BEDŘICH SMETANA (1824–1884)

Smetana ended up suffering from deafness, syphilis and ultimately going completely mad. Before then he made his name as the father of Czech musical nationalism. His most popular piece, *Vltava* from *Má Vlast (My Homeland)* is about the passage of the River Vltava to the sea. His other big hit is the overture to his opera *The Bartered Bride*.

Well, I Never! Smetana, like a number of composers, went deaf in later life. In his *String Quartet No.1*, the violin plays a long high note, which Smetana said was meant to sound like the whistling in his ears.

ALEXANDER BORODIN (1833–1887)

Borodin was only a part-time composer. His day job was as a highly respected scientist in Russia. As a result, his first published work was a scientific paper, rather than a piece of music. His opera *Prince Igor* was actually completed after he had died, by composers Nikolai Rimsky-Korsakov and Alexander Glazunov.

Check out: *Polovtsian Dances* from *Prince Igor* | *In the Steppes of Central Asia* | *On the Action of Ethyl Iodide on Hydrobenzamide and Amarien* (his first work).

Name drop: the musical *Kismet*, which is based on Borodin's tunes.

> *I believe in Bach, the Father, Beethoven, the Son, and Brahms, the Holy Ghost of music.*
> **HANS VON BÜLOW, CONDUCTOR AND PIANIST**

JOHANNES BRAHMS (1833–1897)

Now known to many as one half of the rhyming slang for 'drunk', in his early career Brahms earned a living playing piano in brothels around his native Hamburg. He continued to tour as a pianist and was regarded as a master of every type of music, except for opera, to which he never turned his hand. Brahms may have been musical in the daytime, but at night his snoring was a far from sweet sound. One conductor, forced to share a room with him, described how 'the mostly unearthly noises issued from his nasal and vocal organs'.

Brahms would never have won the award for 'best-turned-out composer'. He seems to have had particular problems in the trouser department. He hated buying new clothes and often wore baggy trousers which were covered in patches and nearly always too short. Once, his trousers nearly fell down altogether in the middle of a performance. On another occasion, he took a tie from around his neck and looped it around his waist in place of a belt.

Brahms wrote his *Academic Festival Overture* to celebrate being given an honorary degree by the University of Bremen. At its first performance, the largely student audience were delighted to hear the tune to their favourite student song *Gaudeamus Igitur* included in the music. It's said that they cheered and threw their hats in the air.

Check out: *Hungarian Dance No. 5* | *Piano Concerto No. 1* | *Symphony No. 4* | *Violin Concerto.*

Name drop 1: Clara Schumann. Brahms was quite besotted with her, and probably wanted the relationship to go further after her husband Robert had died.

Name drop 2: Johann Strauss II. Despite the difference in their music, these two were firm friends. When Mrs Strauss once asked Brahms for an autograph, he wrote out a few bars of *By the Beautiful Blue Danube*, with the note 'Sadly, not by Brahms!'

> *I played over the music of that scoundrel Brahms. What a giftless bastard! It annoys me that this self-inflated mediocrity is hailed as genius.*
> **PETER ILYICH TCHAIKOVSKY, COMPOSER**

> On his way out of a party:
> *If there is anyone here whom I have not insulted, I beg his pardon.*
> **JOHANNES BRAHMS, COMPOSER**

Orders for Matilda's composer-themed weather vane always seemed to flood in when she wore her favourite party frock.

CAMILLE SAINT-SAËNS (1835–1921)

To say that Saint-Saëns was a clever kid is an understatement. This book is full of child stars, but he was probably the most prodigious of the lot. He could read and write and play tunes on the piano at the age of just two. By the age of seven he was something of an expert in lepidoptery (the study of butterflies to us mere mortals). His best-known piece is *Carnival of the Animals,* which he banned from being performed during his lifetime in case people stopped taking him seriously. The animal theme continues, albeit unwittingly, with his other famous work, his *'Organ' Symphony No. 3,* which will forever be linked to 'sheep-pigs', after being used in the film *Babe.*

Check out: *Violin Sonata No. 1* | *Danse Macabre* | *Mon coeur s'ouvre à ta voix,* from his opera *Samson and Delilah* – a contender for most beautiful aria ever.

DOUBLE BASS

Only the harp rivals this giant as the most difficult orchestral instrument to fit in the back of an estate car. Composers often use the deep sound of the double bass not just for its low, sonorous effect but also to add a little light relief to their music. For example, in Saint-Saëns' *Carnival of the Animals,* it plays the part of the elephant - another thing that it's difficult to get in the back of an estate car.

Check out: *Double Bass Concerto* by Karl Ditters von Dittersdorf. Crazy name, crazy guy.

Name drop: Serge Koussevitsky, legendary conductor with the Boston Symphony Orchestra, was a virtuoso double bass player.

LÉO DELIBES (1836–1891)

The Delibes opera *Lakmé* soared to new heights of popularity on the back of the long-running British Airways advertising campaign, which features the opera's most famous tune, the *Flower Duet.* His other popular composition is the ballet *Coppélia,* which tells the story of a toymaker and his dancing doll.

Check out: The ballet *Sylvia.*

Name drop: Berlioz and Bizet, both of whom were Delibes' bosses when he was chorus master at Paris's Théâtre Lyrique.

FAMOUS BALLETS: WHAT IS ACTUALLY GOING ON?

NO. 2: DELIBES: *COPPÉLIA*
(OR... *GOT MYSELF A DANCING, SWEATING,*
PIROUETTING LIVING DOLL)

Delibes based his ballet on the book *Der Sandmann* by the German novelist, E.T.A. Hoffmann, whose first names were Ernst Theodor Amadeus (the last changed in honour of Mozart). *Coppélia*, which is subtitled *The Girl with the Enamel Eyes* – i.e. doll – was first performed at the Paris Opera in May 1870. The classic tale, not unlike Pygmalion, quickly went around the world in a wave of popularity. These days, it still manages to preserve its place in the ballet top ten, although the original practice of casting one of the central male characters, Franz, as a woman – a custom known as 'en travestie' in the ballet world – has now all but died out.

Act 1

We open in a dull, peasant village. The villagers are currently holding a huge festival to celebrate the fact that they have just taken delivery of a new town bell. Told you it was a dull village. Events are further enlivened by the fact that, according to the age old traditions of Dullsville, anyone who wants to get married during the festival will be rewarded with money. As you can imagine, there's an unseemly rush to get hitched. The lovely Swanilda – clearly a cross between a Tchaikovsky heroine and a Wagner one – wants to bag local klutz, Franz. They talk love, but she remains unconvinced that his is true. Missing the chance to shout 'Hit it, Joe!' at the orchestra's conductor before serenading her with a round of 'SWANEE... how I love ya, how I love ya...', he opts for the classic hurt puppy look. To be honest, Swanilda's pretty sure he's more enraptured with the motionless female figure on the nearby balcony, than he is with her. She challenges him with another local tradition. She will hold an ear of wheat to her ear. If it rattles, it means he loves her. If there's no rattle, he doesn't. (We did tell you this town was dull. Maybe this is what they did before television was invented). She does the wheat thing – no rattle. He does it, and insists there was a rattle.

The scene is interrupted by the mad figure of Dr Coppelius leaving his house – it's the one with the motionless female figure on the balcony. He's mobbed by local kids and in the confusion, Dr Coppelius drops his house keys. Swanilda nabs them and decides to partake in a spot of breaking and entering, so keen is she to get the lowdown on the mysterious woman on the balcony. At the same time, unbeknownst to her, Franz has a similar plan. But, being the Alpha Male of the outfit, he decides on the Romeo route: straight up the grapevine and in through the balcony window.

Act 2

Swanilda has done a deal with her girlfriends. Instead of a Saturday night spent sitting outside the local corner shop, barracking anyone who enters, they have broken into Dr C's house. They find themselves in a room full of female forms, each one eerily motionless and with a vacant expression. They prove to be dolls as does, to Swanilda's relief, the woman on the balcony. When Swanee and the girls wind them up, they start to move in stilted, awkward motions to strange, spooky music. Suddenly, Dr C returns home and discovers them. They don't think to ask how he got in the door considering they have the key but, instead, run screaming to the exit. Swanilda, however, stays behind and hides, keen to see what other weird goings-on go on are weirdly going on, in the house of Dr C.

Just at that point, Franz enters from the balcony. Dr C greets him with open arms and offers him a G and T, laced with sleeping drugs. Not in the least surprised to be greeted with an aperitif rather than an Asbo (he's possibly a few clowns short of a circus, young Franz), he sups and then dozes off.

As Swanilda watches from her hiding place, Dr C explains – through a cross between ballet, mime and that moment in the James Bond movie when the villain details *all* their wicked intentions – that he plans to use Franz as a human sacrifice to bring the doll on the balcony – who he has rather disturbingly called Coppélia – to life. Turns out, he loves his dolls, yes, but… well, gripping hands and real hair is no longer good enough. He wants the living, breathing, real deal. As he is getting a magic spell ready, Swanilda dresses up in Coppélia's clothes and pretends to be the doll, come to life. Dr C is over the moon and he nips off to get his camera.

Swanilda revives her groggy beau. In his stupor, he tells her she 'is his best mate and that, no… no… listen… I really mean it.' She, meanwhile, has set all the dolls going again, and, as Dr C comes back to face the dancing chaos, she and Franz nip off to safety. The curtain closes on Dr C, staring sadly at the real Coppélia, who now lies forlorn, with no visible signs of life.

Act 3

The curtain reopens on the town square. The Festival of the New Town Bell (hurrah!) is in full swing and going like the clappers. Swanilda and Franz, no doubt having put Franz's previous desires for an automaton behind them, are about to say 'I do', when the raging Dr C appears. For some strange reason, Swanilda feels bad about the mess she caused by setting all the dolls off – Dr C's attempted murder of her betrothed clearly not being an issue. She offers Dr C her dowry, by way of recompense. Is she mad? At this point, her Dad steps in. He tells her to keep the dowry, and he will pay off the murderous Dr C. Are they all mad? Dr C accepts (NO!) and everyone is happy, if a little deluded. The entire town celebrates by, yes, you guessed it, dancing.

The ballet in brief: *Pygmalion* meets *Peter Grimes*, set during the 80s 'robot dance' craze.

Moral of the story: Before declaring undying love, always check for a pulse. Oh, and who said that crime doesn't always pay?

---

10 CLASSICS USED IN TV ADVERTS:

Bach: *Air on the G String* – Hamlet Cigars
Delibes: *Flower Duet* from *Lakmé* – British Airways
Dvořák: *Symphony No. 9* – Hovis Bread
Einaudi: *Le Onde* – John Lewis
Elgar: *Cello Concerto* – Buxton Natural Mineral Water
Orff: '*O fortuna*' from *Carmina Burana* – Old Spice
Puccini: '*Nessun dorma*' from *Turandot* – Benylin
Rimsky-Korsakov: *Flight of the Bumblebee* – Lurpak
Tchaikovsky: *Dance of the Reed Flutes* – Cadbury Fruit & Nut
Verdi: *Anvil Chorus* from *Il Trovatore* – Ragú Pasta Sauce

GEORGES BIZET (1838–1875)

Another romantic Frenchman. His best-known work is the opera *Carmen*. It tells the story of a beautiful woman who not only seduces a soldier, only to dump him for a matador, but who also works in a cigarette factory. Despite the popularity of *Carmen,* it's another work of Bizet's which is the Classic FM listeners' favourite duet of all time, *'Au fond du temple saint',* from his opera *The Pearl Fishers.*

Check out: *L'Arlésienne Suite No. 1* | *Jeux d'enfants* – ten piano pieces, five of which Bizet wrote out for orchestra.

FAMOUS OPERAS: WHAT IS ACTUALLY GOING ON?

NO. 7: BIZET: *CARMEN* (OR *SMOKE GETS IN YOUR ARIAS*)

Poor Bizet. He died before Carmen had become a hit. And it wasn't as if it happened hundreds of years later. When he died, it was flopping, nightly. Then, for some reason, a mere handful of performances later, it was being hailed as 'sensational'. Now, it's among the most performed operas in the world, even since the smoking ban.

∞ THE PLOT ∞

Act 1

It's Seville, 1830, and boy, is it hot. It's hot outside in the town square, and it's even hotter inside the factory, where the gypsy Carmen and her co-workers make cigarettes all day long. A bunch of soldiers parade across the square. One of them, a corporal called José, tells his lieutenant that the girls in the factory are quite pretty. The factory hooter goes and the largely male crowd watch the parade of girls go past. The girls, for their part, sing beautiful songs … about cigarettes. No lie. (There is no truth in the rumour that Bizet was originally going to call this opera *The Silk Cut Ladder* or *Tales from the Vienna Woodbines*).

82

Carmen leaves the factory and sings her saucy Habanera (a Spanish dance with words). She's positively smokin'. She throws a flower at José, the corporal, and then runs off. José talks to his foster-sister, Micaela, about his mum and about money. Supposedly, José fancies Micaela, but it sure doesn't feel like it.

Suddenly, there's a bit of a fuss coming from the cigarette factory. Someone's been stabbed and the word is it was Carmen who did the deed. José goes into the factory and brings Carmen out. The lieutenant starts to make out her arrest warrant but José, instead of handcuffing her, lets her go, clearly in love with her. End of Act 1 – time for that tuna salad which you brought from home in a Tupperware box to avoid paying opera house prices.

Act 2

We're in a tavern. Carmen and her two gypsy friends are singing. The matador, Escamillo, walks in and quite obviously has the hots for Carmen. She's not interested, though. Neither is she interested in the lieutenant, who tries his luck as well. Gosh, this woman is beating them off with a stick! Turns out, she does want José, after all. He was jailed over the cigarette factory incident, although he's being released from prison today. Suddenly, the pub shuts, and smugglers appear from nowhere. Fantastic – a lock-in. Carmen cries off the smuggling that night, in favour of seducing José. In fact, when he arrives, they get straight down to unfinished business. Sadly, a bugle sounds, which tells him he needs to get back and join the anti-smuggling party. Carmen tries to exert her feminine wiles on him, and, when this fails, resorts to feminine badgering. No need, though, because the lieutenant suddenly walks in. Ah! Tricky one, this. José feels he has no choice but to defend Carmen and fights the lieutenant. Cue the smugglers, who could smell a fight a mile away, and they join in. Oh dear. Looks like José has just left the army and become a smuggler. His family wouldn't consider it a *great* career move. End of act two – have a word with the commissionaire and nip out for a cheeky pint at the pub just up road. That'll be The Kemble's Head (Royal Opera House) or The Welsh Harp (The Coliseum).

Act 3

We're out in the wilds with José, Carmen and the smugglers. José is having the biggest 'what have I done?' moment of his life. Carmen is rapidly going off him. Together with her gypsy girlfriends, she reads her own fortune – you know, just to cheer herself up, because there's never any death in these things, is there? Oh, what's this? Death! What a surprise. Carmen believes it 100%, always having been one for fate. The smugglers and the girls, Carmen included, go off for a quick smuggle and José is left on watch. Micaela, his foster sister, comes looking for him, as does Escamillo, the matador. He says he loves Carmen and Escamillo and José fight. José is winning on points when the smugglers and the girls return. Carmen and Escamillo flash each other one of those 'play your cards right' looks, and he ends up inviting the whole party back to his place in Seville. Micaela suddenly shows herself and begs José to come back to his poor dying mum. Good timing as ever, Mum. What will happen? Act 3 will end, that's what will happen. Time for a... well, as it's Carmen, a nifty cig, stood outside the opera house door.

Act 4

We're in the Bull Ring – Seville, not Birmingham – and this is where it's all going to happen. Escamillo has got his tight trousers and silly hat on, and is strutting his stuff. Carmen is there with Escamillo, all loved up. Her gypsy girlfriends tell her that José is in the crowd, somewhere and he's tooled up. She spies him and goes to talk. They argue over the noise of the crowd and the whole opera climaxes with Carmen throwing her ring at him, and, as the crowd erupts at Escamillo's win over the bull, José stabs Carmen. The crowd close in on him and the curtain closes. So after all that, it wasn't the cigarettes that killed her.

> *As a musician I tell you that if you were to suppress adultery, fanaticism, crime, evil, the supernatural, there would no longer be the means for writing one note.*
> **GEORGES BIZET, COMPOSER**

> *Harpists spend 90 per cent of their lives tuning their harps and 10 per cent playing out of tune.*
> **IGOR STRAVINSKY, COMPOSER**

HARP

It may make a heavenly noise but carrying it is a hell of a job. One of the hardest orchestral instruments to play, the harp nevertheless makes a beautiful sound. When harpists run their fingers all the way across the strings, creating that amazing, dream-like sound, it's called a 'glissando'.

Check out: Mozart: *Flute and Harp Concerto* | Tchaikovsky's *Rose Adagio* opens with a beautiful virtuosic section for harp.

Name drop: The Prince of Wales has recently rekindled the tradition of appointing a harpist to his court. The first of these was Catrin Finch, the second Jemimah Philips and the third, Claire Jones.

Well, I Never! One of Beethoven's string quartets is nicknamed the 'Harp Quartet' because Ludwig wrote glissandos (see above) shared between all four players.

Not to be confused with: Harmonica (mouth organ) players often refer to their instruments as the 'harp'. Don't muddle the two types of harp – it could hurt. While we're on the subject of the harmonica, did you know that every child in Belgium is required by law to take up the instrument while they are at school?

GROUPS OF COMPOSERS

The Mighty Handful (also known as **The Five**) – a group of composers who hailed from the Russian city of St. Petersburg in the second half of the 19th century.

Balakirev

Cui

Borodin

Mussorgsky

Rimsky-Korsakov

Les Six – a group of composers working in France in the 1920s.

Milhaud

Tailleferre

Honegger

Durey

Poulenc

Auric

The Manchester Group – this group of young British composing talent met up while they were studying at the Royal Manchester College of Music (now known as the Royal Northern College of Music).

Peter Maxwell Davies

Harrison Birtwistle

John Ogden

Elgar Howarth

Alexander Goehr

The Second Viennese School – a group of composers who redefined many of the existing rules about classical music at the turn of the 20th century. The first set of famous composers who had a relationship with Vienna included the likes of Mozart, Haydn, Beethoven and Schubert.

Schoenberg

Webern

Berg

MAX BRUCH (1838–1920)

This German composer is best known for his *Violin Concerto No. 1*. It's been voted the UK's favourite piece of classical music no fewer than five times in the annual Classic FM Hall of Fame poll. As well as composing, Bruch spent three years in Liverpool as the Music Director of the Royal Liverpool Philharmonic, now Classic FM's Orchestra in the North-West.

Check out: *Scottish Fantasy | Kol Nidrei.*

ORCHESTRAL FIRST

The Royal Liverpool Philharmonic is the UK's oldest continuously operating professional symphony orchestra. Although the Liverpool Philharmonic Society dates back to 1840, the orchestral musicians were not permanently contracted until 1853, five years ahead of the launch of the next oldest, the Hallé Orchestra, down the road in Manchester.

ON RECORD

In 1998, the Royal Liverpool Philharmonic Orchestra was the first UK orchestra to launch its own record label, *RLPO Live*. The innovation was an initiative of the musicians themselves.

VIRTUAL PERFORMANCE

In September 2007, the Royal Liverpool Philharmonic gave the first ever professional orchestra concert presented live within the virtual online world of *Second Life*. Audience members from across the globe 'sat' in a 3-D virtual version of the orchestra's home venue, the Liverpool Philharmonic Hall. They were able to watch and listen live as Vasily Petrenko conducted the real orchestra in a performance of works by Rachmaninov, Ravel and two contemporary Liverpool composers.

UP IN SMOKE

Liverpool's original Philharmonic Hall was opened in 1849 and burnt to the ground in 1933. The current art deco building, home to the Royal Liverpool Philharmonic Orchestra, was opened in 1939. If you're there, make sure you allow time to nip into the Gents of the Philharmonic pub opposite. The red marble urinals are listed and have become a big attraction for visitors to the city – something of an inconvenience if you happen to be availing yourself of the convenience at the moment when a coach party drops in for a peek.

> " *Truly there would be reason to go mad if it were not for music.*
> **PETER ILYICH TCHAIKOVSKY, COMPOSER** "

PETER ILYICH TCHAIKOVSKY (1840–1893)

One of the greatest of all composers, Tchaikovsky led a tortuous life. He suffered from depression and was suicidal on more than one occasion. He was driven to despair by the poor reception given to his early compositions (many of which are now huge hits) and by guilt over his homosexuality, which was socially unacceptable at the time. His benefactor throughout his life was a rich widow, who insisted they never actually meet. There is confusion over exactly how he died – officially, cholera from infected water claimed his life, although there is some evidence that he may have drunk it knowingly. Tchaikovsky had a knack for great tunes and lots of them. His ballets are among the most often performed today.

Check out: *Nutcracker* | *1812 Overture* | *Piano Concerto No. 1* | *Symphony No. 6 ('Pathétique')* | *Romeo and Juliet* | *The Sleeping Beauty* | *Swan Lake.*

Well, I Never! When Tchaikovsky received his honorary degree from Cambridge University on 13th June, 1893, he was in amazing company. Also receiving degrees that day were Saint-Saëns, Bruch and Puccini's librettist, Arrigo Boito.

OVERTURE

There are two types of overture. Type A - the bit that comes at the beginning of an opera. It's very often a sort of greatest hits showcase of the tunes that will follow. Sometimes, though, composers will write an overture that doesn't have anything else coming afterwards (Type B). Possibly the most famous example of this is Tchaikovsky's *1812 Overture.*

Check out: the overture to Mozart's *The Marriage of Figaro (A)* | Tchaikovsky's fantasy overture from *Romeo and Juliet (B)* | Wagner's overture to *The Flying Dutchman* (A) | Brahms' *Academic Festival Overture (B).*

FAMOUS BALLETS: WHAT IS ACTUALLY GOING ON?

NO. 1: TCHAIKOVSKY: *SWAN LAKE* (OR *S'WANDERFUL*)

Lebedinoe ozero (*The Lake of the Swans*) opened in Moscow at the Bolshoi Theatre on February 27th, 1877. It was, initially, neither a huge hit nor a disaster. After various changes, cuts and tweaks, it has gone on to be one of the most popular ballets of all time. Ironically, Tchaikovsky himself never saw the entire ballet. He only caught a production of the second act, in Prague once in 1888. There are great versions to look out for on film these days, including both a classic Nureyev/Fonteyn production from 1966 and an intriguing *Barbie at the Ballet* version, where an animated version of the Barbie doll plays the lead. Each to their own.

Act 1

It's the night of a huge royal party. Prince Siegfried, who would no doubt be played in the movie by George Clooney, is busy spending his inheritance when he remembers what the reason of the entire gig is in the first place: he has to choose a wife. That's right. After all, it did say on the invite 'The Prince cordially requests the pleasure of your company at a special "Birthday/Choosing-His-Wife" night. Please bring a bottle'. Looking around the sad bunch of shiny debs, the Prince is totally fed up and decides to run off into the night. Out in the forest, he sees a flock of swans glinting in the moonlight. After a quick check over his shoulder for any anti-hunting types, he hot-foots it after them.

Act 2

The Prince creeps up on the swans. They're in the forest, at a lake. They dance – as swans do. The prince licks his lips and thinks 'Mmm... Swan au Vin. Marvellous'. He's about to pick one off with his crossbow when he notices that one of them is remarkably feminine, for a swan. Within seconds, he is lovestruck and dribbling. He approaches her, dances with her and pretty soon, he knows her name, her star-sign and is well on the way to getting a phone number. She is Odette and, every night at midnight, she turns into a human – *again*. You see, it turns out she shouldn't really be a swan at all. She was turned into one by the vile and loathsome Von Rothbart. Let's face it, he was always going to be a bad 'un with a name like that. Even weirder, Odette tells The Prince that the lake, the 'Swan Lake' of the title, was formed out of the tears of her parents, grief-stricken at her plight. The Prince suppresses an urge to yell 'Warning! Bunny-boiler!' and to run for the hills. Instead, he falls in love. Well, why not? The party wasn't up to much and *Britain's Got Talent* hadn't yet been invented. Suddenly, Von Rothbart appears and The Prince rediscovers his macho side, offering to run him through there and then. Odette has to stop him, though. If VR dies, then the spell on her can never be broken. Ah, right. Problem. The Prince has got the length of the interval to figure out a way round it.

Act 3

The Prince is back at his party. He has eschewed the conga line in favour of pacing around and scratching his chin, trying to find the way out of his love problems. Just as he's considering looking up the devil in the phone book, the doors of the ballroom fly open and there stands... Von Rothbart. Cue dramatic chord. With him, as far as The Prince can tell, is Odette. Only, she's all in black, not white. Admittedly, the LBD suits her (and he makes a mental note to tell her later when they're alone) but there's something else that's different. Has she Botoxed, he wonders? He can't quite put his finger on it. Nevertheless, she looks stunning and, never one to look a gift wife in the mouth, he stands on a chair, calls for silence and announces that this wonderful little corker by his side in the cute black number will be his wife. The assembled crowd of liggers and hangers-on don rictus grins and burst into a seemingly spontaneous round of 'For he's a jolly good feudal overlord' (not *usually* included in the Tchaikovsky version).

As the last strains are ringing in his ears, The Prince notices a face at the window. It's Odette – in white. He looks at his betrothed by his side. She smiles. 'The name's Odile, by the way – Odile Von Rothbart. Daughter. And you will cook me breakfast in the morning, won't you?' The Prince is horror struck. He has inadvertently promised to marry the *wrong* swanlike woman, albeit one who looks hot in black. What is he to do? Get a drink, we say. So long as you ordered it beforehand – let's face it, when the ballet fans get a thirst on, some theatre bars can be like Smithfields on Christmas Eve.

Act 4

The Prince runs to the lake and discovers Odette, still in white, and weeping. He quickly switches into 'Please Forgive Me' mode, doing his best to say all the right things. 'I've been so stupid. No, of course I love you. No, I don't want to see other swans. Yes, admittedly, I thought she looked good in black'. Odette forgives him, but no sooner has she put her wings around him than Von Rothbart appears. It gradually dawns on the two lovers that they will never be together unless they take drastic action. As the music plays – their swansong, presumably – they join arms, leap into the lake and sink to their watery deaths. Von Rothbart, now powerless to harm them, dies too. In fact, there's barely a living soul left on the stage. No wonder there's a queue for a drink at the bar.

The ballet in brief: Swan thing leads to another but it's not all white – in fact it's very black indeed.

Moral of the ballet: Don't date outside your species.

FAMOUS BALLETS: WHAT IS ACTUALLY GOING ON?

NO. 2: TCHAIKOVSKY: *NUTCRACKER* (OR *AND HERE IT IS, MERRY CHRISTMAS, EVERYBODY'S GOING NUTS*)

Nutcracker was the third of Tchaikovsky's 'Big Three' ballets, following on from *Swan Lake* and *The Sleeping Beauty*. It was based on E.T.A. Hoffmann's story, *Der Nussknacker und der Mäusekönig*, which translates as *The Nutcracker and the Mouse King*. It received its premiere in December 1892, by which time, Tchaikovsky had already stolen the best bits of music from himself for a little suite and this was proving very popular. The ballet didn't do nearly so well at first, and its place as part of the Christmas routine didn't really start to be established until as late as the 1950s. Maybe post-war Europe needed a little sugar sweet, escapist fantasy. One of the undoubted stars of the show, though, was neither a ballerina nor a tune... it was an instrument. The celesta was one of those instruments that Tchaikovsky simply HAD to have. It was only invented in 1886 and, when Tchaikovsky heard it in France, he wrote letters home about wanting to be the first person in Russia to use it. His wish was granted in his orchestral piece *The Voyevoda*, in 1891.

It's interesting to note that the celesta, which is a sort of glockenspiel built into a small case so that you can play it like a piano, is still used to inspire the same sense of magic and wonder today: think of John Williams' *Harry Potter* soundtracks and, in particular, the amazing celesta sounds used in *Hedwig's Theme*.

Act 1

There's a party going on. There's always a party going on. This time, it's because it's Christmas Eve, and it's at the Stahlbaum's house. Mr and Mrs Stahlbaum have two children, Clara and Fritz. They also have a huge house – one room of which *alone* is as big as the Royal Opera House stage – and a strange line in godfathers. The godfather to their children is called Herr Drosselmeyer. Herr, mind. Not John or Alan or Barry. He's always addressed as 'Herr'. When he enters, he does so with a flourish, producing a huge sack of gifts for all the children. Fritz is given three life size dolls, which can come to life and dance. Nice thought. However, Clara, his sister, is seemingly overlooked and throws a hissy fit. So, Herr Drosselmeyer fumbles in his pockets and comes up with … a nutcracker in the shape of a toy soldier. Most people wouldn't have risked it and would have gone for tokens, but Clara seemed to quite like it. Fritz, though, now sees himself as hard done by. After all, he only got strangely magical, life-size dolls that could defy reason, come alive and dance. 'And she got a nutcracker!' Incensed at the unfairness, not to say weirdness of it all, he too throws a hissy fit and in doing so, breaks the nutcracker. Herr D. repairs it and, after a communal dance – in this instance, it's the traditional Grosvater Tanz but today you might substitute the Macarena – all go to bed.

In the night (remember it's Christmas Eve) Clara wakes up. For 'wakes up' read *begins to dream,* by the way. Sorry, don't want to spoil anyone's fun, but, well, it's about to get daft. Here goes. As the clock strikes midnight, Clara notices there are mice in her room. She tries to run off to the cupboard to fill in her *Springwatch* diary, but the mice stop her. Then, the Christmas tree in her rooms grows to an enormous size, the nutcracker comes to life – as a soldier – and a battle ensues between him and the Mouse King. Limited suspension of disbelief notwithstanding, Clara helps the soldier by standing on the Mouse King's tail allowing the nutcracker to stab him. Please don't worry though: no mice are actually harmed during the making of this ballet. With their leader dead, and no doubt a good deal of confusion about how they all managed to be dragged into this sorry affair in the first place, the mice retreat, leaving Clara alone to witness something rather special: the nutcracker is no longer a nutcracker. He's not even a toy soldier. He's… a Prince.

93

The two decide to travel to another world – via a portal inside the irradiated Christmas tree – and they see dancing snowflakes, as well as fairies and queens. It's starting to appear that E.T.A. Hoffman may well have been the 19th century Timothy Leary. A bewildered audience turns down a drink in favour of a strong coffee.

Act 2

Clara and the Nutcracker-turned-soldier-turned-Prince find themselves at the amazing palace of the Sugar Plum Fairy, in the Land of Sweets. The Land of Sweets will no doubt soon be replaced, in modern performance, by the Land of Five Fruit a Day, but for now, we'll let it pass. Clara and the Prince are treated to dances from various interesting characters, all of whom do their party pieces, including: The Dew Drop Fairy; some Spanish dancers, made of chocolate; some Chinese dancers, made of tea; Arabian dancers, made of coffee; Russian dancers, in the form of candy canes; Mother Ginger and her little Polichinelles or sweets; clowns or buffoons; reed flutes, or Mirlitons; the Sugar Plum Fairy herself; and, finally, some flowers.

Afterwards, Clara and the Prince head back home. After Clara steps through the portal in the giant Christmas tree, she turns to find the Prince, but he has gone. It's probably for the best, love. Next morning, she wakes to find that the nutcracker is just a nutcracker. The aching disappointment is soon forgotten when she realizes that it's Christmas Day.

The ballet in brief: *The Godfather* – meets *Willy Wonka* – on point.

Moral of the ballet: Don't eat cheese close to bedtime.

PREVIOUS LIVES

Tchaikovsky and Schumann both studied to become lawyers before switching to composing full-time. They weren't alone in opting for a career change: Berlioz trained to be a doctor, Borodin was a scientist, Mussorgsky was a civil servant and Rimsky-Korsakov was in the navy from the ages of 12 to 27. César Cui was an engineer by trade and became a highly respected expert on military fortifications. His publications on the subject included the nattily entitled *Size of Fortresses and the Modification of Their Form Depending on the Expansion of the Strength of Armies*.

PERCUSSION

Orchestral instruments that you either hit or shake. They include the timpani (or kettledrums), cymbals, glockenspiel, xylophone, marimba, triangle, tambourine, castanets, tubular bells, side drum and bass drum. The percussion section also provides some of the more unusual sound effects that a composer can ask for, such as car horns, wind machines and car suspension springs.

Check out: The triangle in Liszt's *Piano Concerto No. 1* | The tubular bells in Tchaikovsky's *1812 Overture* | The castanets in Manuel de Falla's *The Three-Cornered Hat*.

Name drop: Evelyn Glennie | Colin Currie | The whole percussion section of the Simón Bolívar Youth Orchestra of Venezuela, who know how to party on stage during a classical music concert better than almost anybody else.

ANTONÍN DVOŘÁK (1841–1904)

Dvořák loved his Czech homeland and was terribly homesick when he moved to the USA for three years in the 1890s. While he was there though, he discovered American folk melodies. These tunes heavily influenced him while he was writing his best-known work, the *New World Symphony (Symphony No. 9)*. For many people in the UK though, the slow movement of this symphony will forever be associated with wholemeal bread and North Yorkshire streets, after it was used in adverts for Hovis.

Away from music, Dvořák was a committed trainspotter. He would practise his hobby at the Franz Josef Station in Prague; it's said he knew the train timetable off by heart. But he was, after all, only living up to his name (remove the middle 'tonindv' from Antonín Dvořák). When he went to work in New York he developed a passion for steam ships. Believe it or not, he also became something of a pigeon fancier while he was in the city.

When Dvořák was once staying in London – to oversee a performance of his *Piano Concerto* at Crystal Palace – he was thrown out of the Athenaeum Club. He'd mistaken it for a coffee house and was immediately evicted.

Check out: *Song to the Moon* from the opera *Rusalka* | *Serenade for Strings* | *Slavonic Dances.*

Well, I Never! Dvořák (and Mrs Dvořák, for that matter) liked to get up very early indeed. When they stayed with composer and organist Charles Villiers Stanford in Cambridge, he was more than a little surprised that, when he woke at 6am, the Dvořáks were already to be found sitting under a tree in his garden.

MUSICAL EXPRESS

Antonín Dvořák wasn't the only composer with a passionate interest in trains. Russian Mily Balakirev worked in an administrative job with the Warsaw Railway company. But this wasn't something he did to make ends meet while he was struggling to get started in the world of music. He made the move late on his life, when he had already proved himself to be a very successful composer and musician.

JULES MASSENET (1842–1912)

Massenet is most famous for a piece of incidental music from an opera – this time, it's the gentle *Meditation* from *Thaïs*. Sadly, as far as we know, he never wrote a 'mass in A', thus depriving the world of Massenet's Mass in A. Which, were it to receive an afternoon performance, would be Massenet's Mass in A matinee.

Check out: *Manon*, fantastic opera using the same story as Puccini's *Manon Lescaut,* but nearly a decade earlier.

OPERETTA DUO CARPETED

The lyricist W.S. Gilbert and the composer Arthur Sullivan were the Andrew Lloyd Webber and Tim Rice of their day, penning a string of blockbusting operetta hits, including *HMS Pinafore* and *The Mikado*. Despite this, they never really got on terribly well, often arguing. The final nail in the coffin for their partnership came not because of 'artistic differences' over a particular song or orchestration. Instead their career-ending moment was an almighty bust-up over – wait for it – how much they should spend on a new carpet at the Savoy Theatre in London.

INCIDENTAL MUSIC

Stretching back to ancient Greek times, incidental music is the fore-runner to the film soundtrack. As with Grieg's music to Ibsen's play *Peer Gynt*, it was often written to add atmosphere to the action on stage or even to fill in the sections where the director thought 'What shall we do in this bit where nothing's going on?' If nothing else, incidental music lets the audience know that now is really not the time to nip out for a choc-ice.

Check out: Mendelssohn: incidental music to *A Midsummer Night's Dream* | Sibelius: *Karelia Suite*, which started life as incidental music to a student play | Bizet: incidental music to Daudet's play *L'Arlesienne*.

EDVARD GRIEG (1843–1907)

Grieg is Norway's most famous musical son, although the Scots could lay some claim to him being one of their own because his Scottish great-grandfather emigrated to Scandinavia after the Battle of Culloden. Many of his tunes contain soaring melodies that evoke his Norwegian home.

Check out: *Piano Concerto* | *Holberg Suite* | *Peer Gynt Suites Nos. 1 and 2* (the first includes the hits *Morning Mood* and *In the Hall of the Mountain King*).

Well, I Never! Grieg was given an honorary degree by Cambridge University in 1894. Straight after the ceremony, he rushed to the post office and sent a telegram to a friend, a physician in Bergen who shared his surname. He signed his telegram 'Doctor Grieg'.

CHARLES-MARIE WIDOR (1844–1937)

During his time, Widor (pronounced Vee Door) was the Wayne Rooney of the organ world – a truly dazzling player. His *Organ Symphony No. 5,* and in particular the *Toccata* which ends it, has become a big part of many wedding ceremonies.

Name drop: The Montgolfier Brothers, the balloon pioneers. Widor was vaguely related, on his mother's side.

ORGAN

Known as 'The King of Instruments', these mighty beasts demand that orchestras and audiences come to them. Many organ performances take place in cathedrals or churches, although there are some concert halls with permanent built-in organs. The organ is played not only with the hands, but also the feet, which get their own 'shoe-sized' keyboard under the main organ console.

Check out: J.S. Bach: *Toccata and Fugue in D minor* | Widor: *Organ Symphony No. 5* | Saint-Saëns: *Organ Symphony.*

Name drop: It's good to have a couple of Brits up your sleeve here and to know which particular organ they would regard as being on their 'home turf'. We'd go for Thomas Trotter, who is the organist at Symphony Hall, Birmingham and Ian Tracey, who has the same role in Liverpool's Anglican Cathedral. You might also like to mention the organ at the Royal Albert Hall, which was overhauled as part of a 21st century make-over for 'the nation's village hall'.

To play the organ properly, one should have a vision of Eternity.
CHARLES-MARIE WIDOR, COMPOSER

NIKOLAI RIMSKY-KORSAKOV (1844–1908)

A Russian naval officer turned music professor, Rimsky-Korsakov is best known for *Scheherezade,* which is based on the story of *The Arabian Nights.* When it came to knowing how to write brilliantly for orchestra, Rimsky-Korsakov was in a league of his own and also made quite a name for himself by arranging the work of other composers. Being a navy man, RK wrote some of his music while at sea. His *Symphony in E flat* was written while stationed off Gravesend in the Thames Estuary.

Check out: *Flight of the Bumblebee* | *Capriccio Espagnol* | *Chant Hindou* from his opera *Sadko.*

Well, I Never! Rimsky-Korsakov's name is mentioned in The Beatles' 1968 film, *Yellow Submarine.*

About the composer, Nikolai Rimsky-Korsakov:
*What a name! It suggests
fierce whiskers stained with vodka!*
THE MUSICAL COURIER

GABRIEL FAURÉ (1845–1924)

Highly regarded for his *Requiem,* one of *the* great choral masterpieces, Fauré is far better known in his homeland, where he is more or less the French Elgar. Both composers had their religious faith tested in later life. Fauré's instrumental music is definitely worth a listen.

Check out: *Pavane* | *Cantique de Jean Racine* | *Dolly Suite.*

Well, I Never! Just like Beethoven, Fauré battled against increasing deafness, and wrote his last few works without being able to hear a thing.

FLUTE

This is at the smaller end of the woodwind family. It's still classed as woodwind even though it's usually made from metal. Among the flute's good points – it's perfect for kids to take up, being small enough to be carried to school. Among the bad points, it's very easy to leave on the bus.

Check out: Mozart: *Flute Concertos* | Debussy: *Syrinx*.

Name drop: Sir James Galway was one of those classical musicians who successfully crossed over into a pop star level of fame during the 1970s and 1980s, not least because of the colour of his instrument. Rather than mere silver, he was known as 'the man with the golden flute'. James Bond, eat your heart out. Today, Emmanuel Pahud is one of the most respected flautists.

> **❝** *I'm a flute player, not a flautist. I don't have a flaut and I've never flauted.*
> **JAMES GALWAY, FLUTE PLAYER** **❞**

HUBERT PARRY (1848–1918)

You can't get a more English sounding name than that of Sir Charles Hubert Hastings Parry, the composer of that most English of tunes, *Jerusalem*. An establishment man through and through, Parry was educated at Eton and Oxford University. Although he was among the most successful composers of his day, writing symphonies, oratorios and a piano concerto, musical immortality has come for him through his coronation anthem *'I was glad'* and his hymn tunes which include *'Dear Lord and Father of Mankind'*. By the way, Parry's famous tune for this hymn is called *Repton*. It's not uncommon for hymn tunes to have completely different names to the actual words of the hymn. That's why there are a number of different tunes that go with different hymns. So, if you have a favourite, then make sure you stipulate.

THE RIGHT WORDS RIGHT NOW

You probably know the tunes to those songs that are sung on big, patriotic occasions, but it's a fair bet that you don't know *all* of the words to these British musical greats:

∞ RULE BRITANNIA ∞
Words: James Thomson. Music: Thomas Arne.

Chorus:
Rule, Britannia! Britannia, rule the waves!
Britons never, never, never shall be slaves.

When Britain first, at heaven's command,
Arose from out the azure main,
This was the charter of the land,
And Guardian Angels sang this strain:

(Chorus)

The nations not so blest as thee
Must, in their turn, to tyrants fall,
While thou shalt flourish great and free:
The dread and envy of them all.

(Chorus)

Still more majestic shalt thou rise,
More dreadful from each foreign stroke,
As the loud blast that tears the skies
Serves but to root thy native oak.

(Chorus)

Thee haughty tyrants ne'er shall tame;
All their attempts to bend thee down
Will but arouse thy generous flame,
But work their woe and thy renown.

(Chorus)

To thee belongs the rural reign;
Thy cities shall with commerce shine;
All thine shall be the subject main,
And every shore it circles, thine.

(Chorus)

The Muses, still with freedom found,
Shall to thy happy coasts repair.
Blest isle! With matchless beauty crowned,
And manly hearts to guard the fair.

(Chorus)

Rule, Britannia! Britannia, rule the waves!
Britons never, never, never shall be slaves.

∽ JERUSALEM ∽
Words: William Blake. Music: Sir Hubert Parry.

And did those feet in ancient time
Walk upon England's mountains green?
And was the holy Lamb of God
On England's pleasant pastures seen?

And did the Countenance Divine
Shine forth upon our clouded hills?
And was Jerusalem builded here
Among these dark Satanic Mills?

Bring me my Bow of burning gold!
Bring me my Arrows of desire!
Bring me my Spear! O clouds, unfold!
Bring me my Chariot of fire!

I will not cease from Mental Fight,
Nor shall my Sword sleep in my hand
Till we have built Jerusalem
In England's green and pleasant land.

Words: Arthur C. Benson. Music: Sir Edward Elgar

Land of Hope and Glory, Mother of the Free,
How shall we extol thee, who are born of thee?
Wider still, and wider, shall thy bounds be set;
God, who made thee mighty, make thee mightier yet!

Truth and Right and Freedom, each a holy gem,
Stars of solemn brightness, weave thy diadem.

Tho' thy way be darkened, still in splendour drest,
As the star that trembles o'er the liquid West.

Throned amid the billows, throned inviolate,
Thou hast reigned victorious, thou has smiled at fate.

Land of Hope and Glory, fortress of the Free,
How may we extol thee, praise thee, honour thee?

Hark, a mighty nation maketh glad reply;
Lo, our lips are thankful, lo, our hearts are high!

Hearts in hope uplifted, loyal lips that sing;
Strong in faith and freedom, we have crowned our King!

HER INDOORS

It's no coincidence that Hubert Parry's *Jerusalem* is the calling-card of the Women's Institute. It was adopted following its association with the Votes for Women movement. And the reason why this pressure group adopted the song? Because Parry's wife was herself a suffragette.

LEOŠ JANÁČEK (1854–1928)

If you ever happen to be seated next to the Moravian Ambassador at a sit-down dinner, then you could do worse than namedrop Janáček. Alongside his Czech mates, Dvořák and Smetana, he flew the flag for his homeland, musically speaking. He was in his fifties before he achieved any real recognition.

Check out: the *Sinfonietta*, which stumped up the opening theme tune for the ultimate school skive television series of the 1970s, *Crown Court | Jenůfa*, his most famous opera.

RUGGERO LEONCAVALLO (1857–1919)

Leoncavallo had a stroke of bad luck when he was writing an opera, which he hoped would launch him on the road to fame and fortune. The trouble was that Puccini got there first with his version of *La Bohème*, and the critics and audiences judged it to be better than Leoncavallo's composition. He did have one notable success, an opera called *Pagliacci*, which includes the tenor aria '*Vesti la giubba*', which continues to be among the most popular of any in the operatic repertoire.

Well, I Never! Queen's 1984 hit *It's a Hard Life* starts with a snippet of '*Vesti La Giubba*', sung to the words 'I don't want my freedom, there's no reason for living...'

EDWARD ELGAR (1857–1934)

One of the greatest British composers, Elgar is quite rightly regarded as a national treasure. He spent much of his life living in his native Worcestershire and the beautiful surrounding English countryside inspired him to write many of the most quintessentially English tunes. And his handlebar moustache is to die for. See for yourself by taking a look at the back of an old-style twenty-pound note. The reason the Royal Mint chose him? The detail on his big bushy moustache would be difficult for counterfeiters to forge.

When Elgar wrote his *Variations on an Original Theme,* it was dubbed the *Enigma Variations* because every movement depicted one of his friends, each of whom was labelled only with initials. The bigger enigma is the identity of the 'original' theme. Some think it's based on a famous tune, some think that it's a well-known melody reversed and altered, others say that the 'enigma' tune is not played but just fits alongside the tune Elgar wrote. Who knows?

Check out: *Cello Concerto* | *Chanson de matin* | *Pomp and Circumstance March No. 1* (the tune to *'Land of Hope and Glory'*) | *Salut d'amour* | *Serenade for Strings.*

Well, I Never! When the composer Dvořák came over to England to conduct his Sixth Symphony in Worcester Shire Hall, one of the rank of first violins was none other than Edward Elgar. Elgar loved the work: '… simply ravishing', he wrote.

LIVE AT ABBEY ROAD

When Abbey Road Studios opened in London in 1931, the first recording ever made there was of Elgar's *Falstaff,* with the composer himself conducting. There's no photo of him walking over the zebra crossing outside, though.

Born in 1879, the composer John Ireland doesn't actually hail from Ireland. He was in fact from England, having been born in Altrincham in Greater Manchester. Just to add to the all round general confusion, his family originally came from Scotland.

CELLO

This string instrument, played between the knees, comes between the viola and double bass in terms of pitch. It's more or less an oversized violin, although you shouldn't try getting one under your chin as the spike would certainly smart a bit. If you imagine the violin, viola, cello and double bass as being roughly the string equivalent of soprano, alto, tenor and bass, respectively, then the cello is the heroic, hunky tenor. By the way, you may see the word cello with an apostrophe at the front of it. This is because the instrument's original full name was violoncello, but these days the 'violon' bit has fallen into disuse except in some orchestral circles.

Check out: Elgar: *Cello Concerto* | Bach: *Cello Suites*.

Name drop: Mstislav Rostropovich | Jacqueline du Pré | Julian Lloyd Webber | Steven Isserlis | Yo-Yo Ma | Guy Johnston | Natalie Clein.

WHAT'S IN A NAME?

The literal translation of the first name of Russian cellist Mstislav Rostropovich is 'avenged glory', although he was known by most of his friends as 'Slava', which simply means 'glory'. Have a listen to one of his recordings and you'll quickly hear why the name is so appropriate.

Said to a female cellist:
*Madam, you have between your legs
an instrument capable of giving pleasure to thousands
– and all you can do is scratch it.*
**SIR THOMAS BEECHAM. ALSO ATTRIBUTED TO
FELLOW CONDUCTOR, ARTURO TOSCANINI**

KEEPING IT IN THE FAMILY

The cellist Julian Lloyd Webber may be the most famous of the Lloyd Webber dynasty when it comes to classical music, but that hasn't stopped his big brother Andrew making incursions from musical theatre into the classical world. His *Requiem* was premiered in 1985 and gave us the enduringly popular *Pie Jesu*. It's not really surprising that both the Lloyd Webbers have done so well for themselves in the music business – their father William was himself a prolific and respected composer. Julian Lloyd Webber has spent many years ensuring that his father's music reaches the audience that it deserves.

GIACOMO PUCCINI (1858–1924)

Puccini took the opera baton from Verdi and ran with it, writing hit aria after hit aria. *La Bohème, Tosca* and *Madam Butterfly* are quite possibly the three most performed operas today. He also penned the aria that, for many people, simply is opera – *'Nessun Dorma'* from *Turandot*. This song, made famous by *The Three Tenors* at the 1990 World Cup Finals in Italy, brought classical music into millions of people's lives.

Whenever Puccini came to London, he always liked to stay at the Savoy, savouring the luxury. On one occasion, in the summer of 1911, he availed himself of the in-house barbers, only to find himself sat in a chair next to Guglielmo Marconi, a fellow Italian and radio pioneer.

Right at the end of *Tosca*, the eponymous heroine meets a rather sudden end by jumping from the parapet of a prison, moments after her lover Mario has met his death at the hands of a firing squad. Usually there's a mattress back stage to lessen the impact of the singer's fall. On more than one occasion, the tragedy has turned to hilarity as the heroine hurls herself off the parapet, only to bounce back into the audience's view.

Puccini himself died before he could finish writing his opera *Turandot*. Another composer wrote the ending. At the premiere, the conductor Arturo Toscanini stopped the orchestra playing exactly at the point where Puccini stopped composing, turned to the audience and said: 'Here, death triumphed over art.'

Check out: *'Che gelida manina'* and *'O soave fanciulla'* from *La Bohème* | *'O mio babbino caro'* from *Gianni Schicchi* | *'Un bel di'* and *The Humming Chorus* from *Madam Butterfly* | *'Vissi d'arte'* from *Tosca*.

Name drop: Franco Alfano, the man who finished off *Turandot* when the composer died leaving it unfinished.

Well, I Never! When Al Jolson wrote his hit song *'Avalon'* in 1920, Puccini was not one of those who found his foot tapping. His publishers, Ricordi, sued Jolson, saying it sounded like Puccini's aria *'E Lucevan le stelle'*, from *Tosca*. They won, and were awarded $25,000 damages along with all future royalties to the song.

FAMOUS OPERAS: WHAT IS ACTUALLY GOING ON?

NO. 8: PUCCINI: *LA BOHÈME* (OR *DO RE MIMI*)

If you haven't ever seen an opera, La Bohème's not a bad place to start. It's a slushy, Sunday afternoon movie with music. If you cried your head off at *An Affair to Remember*, then this is the opera for you.

∾ THE PLOT ∾

Act 1

Rodolfo, the lead, is living in an arty student flat. He's a writer and his flatmates include a painter and a musician. It's Christmas Eve, 1830, and they are so broke that Rodolfo has to use the article he is writing to keep the fire going. Schaunard, his musical flatmate, arrives home with money, and takes everyone out for supper. Rodolfo stays in, to try to write. There's a knock at the door. It's Mimi, who asks him for a light for her candle, which has blown out leaving her in the dark – yeah, right. She has a brief coughing fit, drops her key and they both end up looking for it. Their hands meet and....VOOM! Or should I say, his hand meets her tiny frozen hand and....VOOM! She tells him she's an embroiderer – how romantic. Rodolfo's friends call him to come for supper but he decides to stay and sing songs about Mimi in the moonlight. End of Act 1. Time for a pre-plated prawn sandwich in the bar.

Act 2

Mimi meets everyone. She is introduced to Rodolfo's friends, particularly Marcello (the artist) and Musetta, who fancies Marcello. Musetta does a saucy little slow waltz for Marcello and they cuddle. Everything is going well, apart from the bill for supper, which Musetta manages to get charged to one of her other suitors. End of Act 2. Kettle Chips in foyer.

Act 3

Time has passed. Mimi tells Marcello that Rodolfo is a bit clingy and jealous and she thinks she might dump him. She has another coughing fit. (Either Puccini is trying to tell us something, or he can even see music in an inflamed oesophagus). Rodolfo enters and, indeed, he acts jealous and clingy. Although he suspects she might be unwell, they decide to split up. Meanwhile Marcello gets a little miffed at Musetta's flirting. It's becoming like an episode of *Desperate Housewives*. End of Act 3. Glass of pinot grigio in the crush bar.

Act 4

Back in the flat. Rodolfo is missing Mimi and Marcello is missing Musetta. The whole thing has the air of a student bedsit, minus the repeats of *Bargain Hunt*. Musetta bursts in, frantic. She had found Mimi at the bottom of the stairs, collapsed. Rodolfo rushes off and carries her into the flat. They lay her on the bed and she seems a little better, but very weak. Musetta decides to sell her earrings to raise money for medicine and one of the other flatmates decides to sell his coat. (Possibly the only place in opera where someone sings goodbye to a coat. Honestly). Alone, Mimi and Rodolfo think about happier times together. The others come back and try to help Mimi, but she dies. At first, Rodolfo – at the other side of the room – doesn't realise, but then he works out the looks on the others' faces and just explodes in grief, shouting/singing 'Mimi!' before the curtain closes. What an ending.

> " *I know I have a reputation for bad tempers,*
> *but I am always having good tempers.*
> **MARIA CALLAS, OPERA SINGER** "

IF AT FIRST YOU DON'T SUCCEED...

The story of Puccini's *Madam Butterfly* is a testimony to that old adage, 'If at first you don't succeed, try and try again'. When the original version of the opera had its premiere on February 17th 1904, it was a flop. Puccini had been working on it right up to the wire and the cast and musicians were inadequately rehearsed. Rather than give up on the opera altogether, Puccini gave it a complete overhaul, splitting the original second act into two acts in the process. When it was performed again eleven days later, the new version was a roaring success, which has been performed around the world ever since.

GUSTAV MAHLER (1860–1911)

A renowned conductor during his lifetime, particularly of opera, Mahler only rose to real popularity as a composer during the latter half of the 20th century. He was a tortured soul who was analysed by Freud. His biggest hit is the *Adagietto* from his *Symphony No. 5*. He wrote nine symphonies, which seems to be *the* number to write – Beethoven and Dvořák also wrote nine.

Check out: *Symphony No. 1* (known as *'The Titan'*) | *Symphony No. 2* (*'The Resurrection'*) | *Symphony No. 8* (known as *'The Symphony of a Thousand'* because of the vast number of musicians needed to perform it).

Name drop: Robert Powell, who played Mahler in the 1974 Ken Russell movie.

ANAGRAMS

An anagram of 'Gustav Mahler' is 'M. Ravel's a thug' and if you jumble up the letters in 'Robert Schumann', you arrive at 'Brahms *Nocturne*'. Mix up the component parts of 'Claude Achille Debussy' and you get 'Delius had a blues cycle'. In a different order, the letters of 'Gabriel Fauré', who is known for his *Requiem*, form 'Grief, be aural'.

> **About Mahler's *Symphony No. 2*:**
> *If that was music, I no longer understand anything about the subject.*
> **HANS VON BÜLOW, CONDUCTOR AND PIANIST**

Some of the greatest classical composers didn't hang around when it came to making music in public. The Spanish composer Isaac Albeniz had his first professional engagement at just four years old. Felix Mendelssohn was nine years old when he first appeared before an audience. Wolfgang Amadeus Mozart was six when he went on his first tour, way ahead of César Franck – he didn't go on the road for the first time until the relatively advanced age of eleven.

> About Claude Debussy's *La Mer*:
> *The audience ... expected the ocean,*
> *something big, something colossal, but they*
> *were served instead with some agitated*
> *water in a saucer.*
> **LOUIS SCHNEIDER, COMPOSER**

CLAUDE DEBUSSY (1862–1918)

Debussy saw himself as a very French musician. He was friendly with many of the impressionist painters, which resulted in his work being given an 'impressionist' tag. In fact, he wasn't really doing an impression of anyone – he was an innovator whose musical style paved the way for other 20th century composers. His lover, Gaby, shot herself when he ended their relationship to set up home with his first wife, Rosalie. Gaby survived her suicide attempt. Five years later, he left Rosalie for the woman who would become his second wife. Just like Gaby, Rosalie shot herself and she, too, lived to tell the tale. The moral of the story? Never marry someone who's a good shot.

Check out: *Clair de lune* | *La Mer* | *Prélude à l'après midi d'un faune*.

Well, I Never! Debussy was staying at the Grand Hotel, Eastbourne, in 1905, when he put the finishing touches to *La Mer*.

FREDERICK DELIUS (1862–1934)

Born in Bradford, Delius decided to become a composer in his twenties when he was running an orange plantation in Florida. In his later years he suffered severely from the syphilis which he had picked up when in Paris in the 1890s. He was forced to dictate his music to his scribe, Eric Fenby, without whom we'd have neither lots of the late Delius output, nor any knowledge of the word 'amanuensis'.

Delius's intermezzo *Walk to the Paradise Garden* sounds particularly idyllic, especially coming, as it does, from the opera *A Village Romeo and Juliet*. Sounds idyllic, that is, until you realise that the Paradise Garden is a pub. They're off for a pint!

Check out: *La Calinda* from the opera *Koanga* | *On Hearing the First Cuckoo in Spring* | If you are feeling adventurous, try a live performance of *A Mass of Life*, Delius's choral masterpiece. It's the musical equivalent of going over a waterfall in a barrel. Marvellous.

Namedrop: Ken Russell, who made a film of Delius's life called *A Song of Summer.*

INTERMEZZO

This is the operatic equivalent of your TV screen going all soft focus and a caption reading 'Ten Years Later' appearing. Don't you just hate it when that happens? Well, an intermezzo – which is the Italian word for 'the bit stuck in' – is a piece of orchestral music in the middle of an opera, which is used to show the audience that a period of time has gone by. But, oddly enough, it's nowhere near as annoying as a 'Ten Years Later' caption.

Check out: Mascagni: *Intermezzo* from *Cavalleria Rusticana* | Delius: *Walk to the Paradise Garden* from *A Village Romeo and Juliet*.

PIETRO MASCAGNI (1863–1945)

This Italian One-Hit-Wonder is best known for his opera *Cavalleria Rusticana*. But rather than a famous aria, it's the Intermezzo that is most often heard today. When this opera is performed in full, it tends to be paired up with another One-Hit-Wonder, Leoncavallo's *Pagliacci* – a double act known as *Cav & Pag*.

It's actually down to Mrs Mascagni that Pietro became well known at all. His wife secretly entered *Cavalleria Rusticana* for a competition after the composer himself decided that it wasn't anywhere near good enough to win. It ended up taking top honours and Mr and Mrs Mascagni's lives were transformed by the prize money. The poor old chap never managed to write another hit to rival it though.

Check out: Er, that's it.

FAMOUS OPERAS: WHAT IS REALLY GOING ON?

NO. 9: MASCAGNI: *CAVALLERIA RUSTICANA*
(OR *VERISMO GREATER LOVE*)

Mascagni's only real big hit, *Cavalleria Rusticana* made its composer a fortune, but it was, by all accounts, a fortune that he lost again. It's often called the start of what is known as 'verismo' opera – real life opera, or if you prefer, a soap opera. Verismo composers – Puccini was another – always took subjects that were gritty and 'of their day'. Mascagni's was based on a book by Verga that would have certainly raised eyebrows with its audience with its themes of infidelity and pregnancy. It won Mascagni a prize for the best one act opera in 1889. As a result, of course, there's no interval, so you'll have to take a snack in your pocket and eat it while nobody's looking. Chocolate is a bad idea and so are crisps.

∽ THE PLOT ∾

It's Easter, in a Sicilian village. Santuzza, a young girl, doorsteps Mamma Lucia and asks her about her son, Turridu. He's gone off to another village to get wine, she is told. But someone saw him in the village, during the night. Mamma Lucia says she'd better come inside. What Santuzza is not telling Mamma Lucia is that she is pregnant.

Alfio plods in, with his horse and cart. He is the village carter and, just to prove it, sings a jolly little song about how lovely it is to be a village carter. It also mentions how lovely it is being married to Lola. (There is no truth in the rumour that Mascagni deleted the lines 'Le sue labbra erano come la cola di ciliegia' – or 'her lips were like cherry cola'). Alfio asks Mamma Lucia for wine, but is told Turridu has gone off for more. Alfio, too, says he saw Turridu not far from his house, this morning. Mmm. Curiouser and curiouser. Santuzza and Mamma Lucia exchange glances. Alfio goes off on his way, and Santuzza leads everyone in the Easter Hymn. No sign of eggs, though. Then after badgering from Mamma Lucia, she spills her guts and explains what's been going on. Turridu had loved Lola, but then he went off to war. Lola married Alfio. When Turridu came back from the war, he started seeing Santuzza. She fell pregnant, but he still loves Lola and sees her whenever Alfio is off, 'carting'.

Turridu enters. Santuzza has a go at him for saying he was off buying wine when he was actually off with Lola. Turridu says he will be toast if Alfio

116

finds out, and Santuzza is then a bit scared for him. Sadly, despite it all, she doesn't want to lose him. Lola comes by, and sings her way into church. Turridu, despite Santuzza's best begging efforts, follows her in, but not before Santuzza has cursed him. When Alfio comes in, then, Santuzza is more than happy to spill the beans about what's been going on.

At this point, there's an 'intermezzo' – literally, a bit stuck in. In the case of *Cavalleria Rusticana*, it's probably the most famous 'bit stuck in' in opera history, and is one of the keys to the opera's success. It is, quite simply, a fantastic tune.

When the congregation come out of church, Turridu is on a high, with Lola by his side. They go off, with friends, to drink wine in Mamma Luccia's trattoria. They continue to drink wine and sing about drinking wine, until Alfio appears. Things get tense and Alfio confronts Turridu. The challenge takes the traditional Sicilian form of an embrace, with Turridu biting Alfio's ear. Don't ask. Smacks of Mike Tyson, but apparently it's a way of saying 'ok, I accept your challenge' in Sicilian.

Turridu goes to see his mum and tells her he's going away and might be some time. If he doesn't come back, in fact, could she look after Santuzza? He leaves just as Santuzza enters, with lots of people from the village. They are all comforting each other when, in a piercing scream, someone yells from outside that Turridu has been murdered. Santuzza faints, and the curtain comes down.

After hearing an opera by another composer:
*I like your opera – I think
I will set it to music.*
LUDWIG VAN BEETHOVEN, COMPOSER

RICHARD STRAUSS (1864–1949)

No relation to the Viennese Strauss family, Richard Strauss is best known for *Also sprach Zarathustra,* which was used in the Stanley Kubrick film *2001: A Space Odyssey.* He is regarded as one of the last great German romantics despite the fact that he was writing well into the 20th century. His international standing fell when he decided to continue working in Germany after 1939, although at the end of the Second World War he was acquitted of being a Nazi collaborator.

Strauss was extremely skilled in the then popular card game of 'Scat' and would often win huge amounts of money playing the game. On one occasion, he had fleeced so much from virtually all the Bayreuth Orchestra that they refused to go on and perform until Winifred Wagner, Richard Wagner's daughter-in-law, had reimbursed them.

Check out: *Der Rosenkavalier* | *Four Last Songs.*

Well, I Never! Strauss was said to be henpecked by his wife, Pauline, a one-time soprano. When she got too much for him at one particular rehearsal, he got his revenge by shouting the last line of his opera, *Salome:* 'Kill that woman!'

 I may not be a first-rate composer, but I am a first-class second-rate composer.
RICHARD STRAUSS, COMPOSER

HOW TO BE A CONDUCTOR

Richard Strauss wrote these *Ten Golden Rules For the Album of a Young Conductor* in 1920:

1. Remember that you are making music not to amuse yourself, but to delight your audience.

2. You should not perspire when conducting: only the audience should get warm.

3. Conduct *Salome* and *Elektra* as if they were by Mendelssohn: Fairy Music.

4. Never look encouragingly at the brass, except with a brief glance to give an important cue.

5. But never let the horns and woodwinds out of your sight. If you can hear them at all they are still too strong.

6. If you think that the brass is now blowing hard enough, tone it down another shade or two.

7. It is not enough that you yourself should hear every word the soloist sings. You should know it by heart anyway. The audience must be able to follow without effort. If they do not understand the words they will go to sleep.

8. Always accompany the singer in such a way that he can sing without effort.

9. When you think you have reached the limits of *prestissimo*, double the pace.

10. If you follow these rules carefully you will, with your fine gifts and your great accomplishments, always be the darling of your listeners.

PASSING THE BATON

Without doubt, conductors are a breed apart from the rest of the orchestra. Not only are they paid thousands of pounds for each appearance, but the top ones tend to spend most of their time either sitting in an airport departure lounge waiting for a flight to their next engagement or twiddling their thumbs in an anonymous hotel in one European city or another. It's no wonder that their arrival in the concert hall for rehearsals tends to be treated by orchestra managers as being only one down from a visit by a member of the Royal Family. It probably also explains why conductors over the years have had one or two prescient things to say about the orchestras with which they perform. So, they get a section of quotations all of their own:

There are two golden rules for an orchestra: start together and finish together. The public doesn't give a damn what goes on in between.
SIR THOMAS BEECHAM, CONDUCTOR

I am not interested in having an orchestra sound like itself. I want it to sound like the composer.
LEONARD BERNSTEIN, CONDUCTOR AND COMPOSER

Said to a member of an orchestra:
God tells me how the music should sound, but you stand in the way!
ARTURO TOSCANINI, CONDUCTOR

> *A good conductor ought to be a good chauffeur.*
> *The qualities that make the one also make the other. They are*
> *concentration, an incessant control of attention, and presence of mind –*
> *the conductor only has to add a little sense of music.*
> **SERGEI RACHMANINOV, COMPOSER**

> To members of his orchestra, who were not performing well:
> *After I die I shall return to earth as the doorkeeper of a bordello,*
> *and I won't let one of you in.*
> **ARTURO TOSCANINI, CONDUCTOR**

> *You know why conductors live so long? Because we perspire so much.*
> **SIR JOHN BARBIROLLI, CONDUCTOR**

> *The conductor has the advantage of not seeing the audience.*
> **ANDRÉ KOSTELANETZ, CONDUCTOR**

KARAJAN CARRY ON

The German conductor Herbert von Karajan is acknowledged as being among the greatest baton-wavers of all time, but he ran his rehearsals in a highly dictatorial style. This joke almost certainly started out life among the ranks of one or orchestra or another, after a particularly demanding rehearsal:

What's the difference between God and von Karajan?
God doesn't think He's a conductor.

JEAN SIBELIUS (1865–1957)

He may have looked like a rather grumpy Kojak, with his shaven head and
lollipop, but in his native Finland he was a musical hero. Many of his best-
loved works are heavily influenced by the folk music of his homeland. He
liked to drink and to smoke and was diagnosed as suffering from throat
cancer in his forties. The operations to remove the malignant growths
were successful and he survived for another half a century. More than
twenty years before he died, having made enough money to live
comfortably, he simply stopped composing and retired. Oh, and we lied
about the lollipop.

Check out: *Karelia Suite | The Swan of Tuonela | Finlandia | Valse Triste |
Violin Concerto | Symphony No. 5.*

Name drop: The Vienna Philharmonic Orchestra. Sibelius was desperate
to be a violin player as much as a composer and he auditioned with them
in 1891. Sadly, he never made the grade, so had to settle for writing one
of the greatest violin concertos in the world.

FRENCH HORN

A member of the brass family, if this instrument is uncoiled it would not only stretch for more than three metres, it would also give you something to do on a Sunday afternoon. Best not attempted during the quiet bit in a concert, though. Great composers for the horn include Mozart and Richard Strauss.

Check out: Mozart: four *Horn Concertos* | Weber: *Concertino for Horn* | Richard Strauss: *Horn Concerto* – possibly for the more adventurous (his father was a horn player in Wagner's orchestra).

Name drop: The greatest horn player in living memory is widely acknowledged to be Dennis Brain, who was killed in a car crash in 1957 at the tragically young age of 36.

ALEXANDER GLAZUNOV (1865–1936)

Glazunov's influence on Russian music was greater than just the sum total of his own work. He studied with Rimsky-Korsakov when he was just a teenager and counted Prokofiev, Stravinsky and Shostakovich among his own pupils later in life.

Check out: *The Seasons* | If you're feeling braver, his one movement *Alto Saxophone Concerto* is fab.

Before I compose a piece, I walk around it several times, accompanied by myself.
ERIK SATIE, COMPOSER

ERIK SATIE (1866–1925)

This French composer is best known for his *Gymnopédies Nos. 1* and *3* for piano. He was something of an eccentric and had a habit of giving many of his compositions ridiculous names.

His strangely titled pieces include: *Veritable Flabby Preludes (for a Dog)* | *Sketches and Exasperations of a Big Boob Made of Wood* | *Five Grins or Mona Lisa's Moustache* | *Menus for Childish Purposes* | *Three Pear-Shaped Pieces* | *Waltz of the Chocolate with Almonds.* He also wrote a remarkable piano piece called *Vexations* which is made of the same few bars of music which are played again and again and again – a total of 840 times.

He was not beyond giving rather odd instructions to performers at the start of his works either. One piano piece was marked 'To be played with both hands in the pocket'.

Check out: Satie's *Three Gnossiennes* | *Parade,* mad ballet music, perfect for putting on when you've come home merry after a night on the razz.

Toscanini's lunchtime vindaloo brought the final movement to a quicker conclusion than either he or the orchestra had anticipated.

MUSICAL MADNESS

There is no better glimpse into the mind of Erik Satie than this timetable of his daily routine published in his *Memoirs of an Amnesiac*:

An artist must organize his life. Here is the exact timetable of my daily activities.

I rise at 7.18, am inspired from 10.23 to 11.47. I lunch at 12.11 and leave the table at 12.14. A healthy ride on horse-back round my domain follows from 1.19 pm to 2.53 pm. Another bout of inspiration from 3.12 to 4.07 pm. From 4.27 to 6.47 pm various occupations (fencing, reflection, immobility, visits, contemplation, dexterity, swimming, etc.)

Dinner is served at 7.16 and finished at 7.20 pm. From 8.09 to 9.59 pm symphonic readings (out loud). I go to bed regularly at 10.37 pm. Once a week, I wake up with a start at 3.19 (Tuesdays).

My only nourishment consists of food that is white: eggs, sugar, grated bones, the fat of dead animals, veal, salt, coco-nuts, chicken cooked in white water, fruit-mould, rice, turnips, camphorised sausages, pastry, cheese (white varieties), cotton salad, and certain kinds of fish (without their skin). I boil my wine and drink it cold mixed with the juice of the fuchsia. I am a hearty eater, but never speak while eating, for fear of strangling myself.

I breathe with care (a little at a time). I very rarely dance. When walking, I clasp my sides, and look steadily behind me.

My expression is very serious; when I laugh it is unintentional, and I always apologize most affably.

I sleep with only one eye closed, very deeply. My bed is round, with a hole to put my head through. Once every hour a servant takes my temperature and gives me another.

I have subscribed for some time to a fashion magazine. I wear a white cap, white stockings, and a white waistcoat.

My doctor has always told me to smoke. Part of his advice runs: 'Smoke away, dear chap; if you don't someone else will.'

RALPH VAUGHAN WILLIAMS (1872–1958)

The music of Ralph Vaughan Williams is as English as warm beer and cricket on the village green. Born in Gloucestershire, he collected traditional English folk songs from a young age and it's these tunes which went on to provide him with the core of many of his subsequent hits. He studied at the Royal College of Music in London, where he sat just a couple of desks along from another great British composer, one Gustav Holst. Since Classic FM began broadcasting in 1992, the popularity of Vaughan Williams has grown steadily each year, with his *The Lark Ascending* topping the annual Classic FM Hall of Fame each year from 2007 to 2009.

Ralph Vaughan Williams wasn't the only famous name in his family – his great uncle was none other than Charles Darwin. By the way, 'Ralph', in this instance is pronounced to rhyme with 'safe', as in the actor Ralph Fiennes.

Check out: *Fantasia on a Theme of Thomas Tallis* | *English Folksongs Suite* | *Fantasia on Greensleeves* | *Symphony No. 2 ('London')*.

Name drop: Down Ampney, the name of the village in Gloucestershire where RVW was born and lived 'til he was two and a bit.

> *Listening to the fifth symphony of Ralph Vaughan Williams is like staring at a cow for 45 minutes.*
> **AARON COPLAND, COMPOSER**

SERGEI RACHMANINOV (1873–1943)

Rachmaninov was one of those annoying people who wasn't just brilliant at one thing – he was top of the pile in three different areas. Today, we remember him as a composer, but in his day he was a fine conductor and magnificent concert pianist. He was already well-known as a performer when he moved to America, but once he had made the States his home, his international superstardom became truly stratospheric. He made enough money to build a house in Los Angeles that was an exact replica of his original home back in Moscow.

Rachmaninov's *Piano Concerto No. 2* has regularly been voted number one in the Classic FM Hall of Fame and his *Piano Concerto No. 3* shot to stardom after being included in the film *Shine*. He's also known for having one of the largest pairs of hands in classical music, which is why some of his piano pieces are fiendishly difficult for less well-endowed performers. He could cover twelve piano keys from the tip of his little finger to the tip of his thumb. That's around four keys more than average.

Rachmaninov was once giving a recital in New York with fellow composer Fritz Kreisler. The former was on the piano and the latter on the violin. Kreisler got into a muddle about where he'd got to in the music. Panic-stricken, he whispered to Rachmaninov, 'Where are we?' The whispered reply came back from Rachmaninov: 'Carnegie Hall'.

Despite his success, Rachmaninov seldom smiled in the photographs he left behind. Perhaps the Russians have no word for 'cheese'. Tall and severe, he was once dubbed 'a six foot scowl'.

Check out: *Rhapsody on a Theme of Paganini* | *Symphony No. 2* | *Vocalise.*

Name drop: *Lorelei*, the name Rachmaninov gave to his car. The composer was mad about cars (and later speedboats) and he was the first in his neighbourhood to have an automobile.

*Never compose anything unless
not composing it becomes a positive
nuisance to you.*
GUSTAV HOLST, COMPOSER

COMPOSERS AND THEIR INSTRUMENTS

Bach – organ, violin and keyboard
Berlioz – flute and guitar
Borodin – flute
Britten – viola
Delius – violin
Dvořák – violin, viola and organ
Elgar – organ, violin and piano
Glinka – piano and voice
Grainger – piano
Holst – trombone
Hummel – piano
Johann Strauss Jr – violin and viola
Khachaturian – tuba
Lehár – violin
Lully – guitar, violin and voice
Nielsen – trumpet
Offenbach – cello
Respighi – violin and viola
Rossini – piano, viola, horn and voice
Sibelius – violin
Smetana – violin and piano
Suppé – flute
Telemann – violin, zither, oboe and organ
Verdi – organ and piano
Vivaldi – violin
Weber – guitar and piano

SIGN LANGUAGE

You know those house signs that you occasionally see which are an amalgamation of the names of the couple living inside? So, 'Marron', for example, probably means that Margaret and Ron live there. Well, genius though he was, Rachmaninov was not above doing it, too. His house on the edge of Lake Lucerne was called 'Senar', which was short for **SE**rgei and **NA**talya **R**achmaninov.

> ❝ *The prospect of having to sit through one of his extended symphonies or piano concertos tends, quite frankly, to depress me. All those notes, and to what end?*
> **AARON COPLAND ON HIS FELLOW COMPOSER, SERGEI RACHMANINOV** ❞

CLARINET

This is the most mellow of the woodwind instruments in the orchestra. When jazz and classical music meet, there's often a clarinet to be found somewhere towards the front of things. A modern clarinet has around 20 keys. Spare a thought for a clarinet player at the time when Mozart wrote his *Clarinet Concerto*. Back then, the clarinet had just six keys. The clarinettist had to play all the same notes a player does today, but with 14 fewer keys.

Check out: Mozart: *Clarinet Concerto* | Copland: *Clarinet Concerto* | The start of the 2nd movement of Rachmaninov's *Symphony No. 2* | Gershwin: *Rhapsody in Blue*.

Name drop: The late Jack Brymer became famous as the LSO's principal clarinettist from 1971 until his retirement. Today, Emma Johnson is one of the most successful British clarinet players.

TUBA

They're big, they're bold and they're brassy. But enough about tuba players. This enormous instrument tends not to be the star of the show, instead operating in a 'Best Supporting' role.

Check out: Vaughan Williams: *Tuba Concerto* – one of the few occasions when the tuba takes centre stage.

Name drop: The composer Aram Khachaturian, who was that rare beast – a composer and a tuba player | Other than that, you can get away with namedropping Tubby.

> *The tuba is certainly the most intestinal of instruments – the very lower bowel of music.*
> **PETER DE VRIES, WRITER, *THE GLORY OF THE HUMMINGBIRD* (1974)**

TROMBONE

The sliding metal tube on a trombone not only lengthens or shortens the pipework to give the instrument a different pitch, it also gives it its 'comedy' value, providing that somewhat *Carry On...* sound. They are the powerhouses of the brass section of the orchestra.

Check out: The trombone was first used in a symphony by Beethoven in his *Symphony No. 5*.

Name drop: Ian Bousefield (principle trombone with the Vienna Philharmonic Orchestra) | Christian Lindberg.

GUSTAV HOLST (1874–1934)

Gustav Holst is most famous for writing *The Planets*. Six of the seven movements represent the astrological influences of the planets: *Mars* (war), *Venus* (peace), *Jupiter* (jollity), *Uranus* (magic), *Saturn* (old age) and *Neptune* (mysticism). The other movement is reserved for *Mercury*, the winged messenger of the gods. Pluto fails to make the line up, mainly because it had not yet been discovered and is not really a planet anyway. The great hymn and rugby anthem *'I vow to thee my country'* is sung to the tune of *Jupiter*.

Check out: *The St. Paul's Suite,* which Holst wrote for his pupils at St. Paul's Girls' School in London, where he was Director of Music for nearly thirty years.

Well, I Never! Despite being viewed now as almost quintessentially English, Holst felt forced to change from Gustavus von Holst to simply Gustav Holst, to offset the German sounding nature of his name, during the First World War.

PLAYING FOR SCOTLAND

The Royal Scottish National Orchestra began its life as the orchestra of the Glasgow Choral Union. It became the Scottish Orchestra in 1891 and the Scottish National Orchestra in 1950. In 1990, Royal status was conferred on the orchestra and it became the Royal Scottish National Orchestra. The composer Gustav Holst was once the orchestra's second trombone. At the time, the band was conducted by another famous composer, Richard Strauss.

FAMOUS DADS

The father of David McCallum (Illya Kuryakin in *The Man from UNCLE*) was the leader of the Royal Scottish National Orchestra in the 1930s. The father of Lonnie Donegan, the king of skiffle, was a violinist in the orchestra at around the same time.

MAURICE RAVEL (1875–1937)

A whole generation of people came across Ravel's music for the first time when Torvill and Dean skated their way to a gold medal accompanied by the *Boléro*. During the First World War, Ravel enlisted as an ambulance driver. He was deeply affected by the death and destruction that he witnessed, and the poignant *Le tombeau de Couperin* was his tribute not only to the French composer Couperin, but also to his fallen comrades.

Check out: *Pavane pour une infante défunte* | The ballet *Daphnis and Chloé* | *Piano Concerto for the left hand* which was written for a friend who lost an arm in the First World War.

Name drop: Belvédère, Ravel's home near Paris, which was his pride and joy.

WAXING LYRICAL

We have the Hungarian composers Béla Bartók and Zoltán Kodály to thank for preserving a whole host of their native folk tunes. They spent years travelling around their homeland recording peasants singing tunes which had been handed down from generation to generation. Their wax cylinder recording equipment wasn't exactly hi-fi, but nevertheless they left musicologists an incredibly valuable record of local music.

IGOR STRAVINSKY (1882–1971)

One of the great composers of the 20th century, this Russian caused a storm during his lifetime because of the innovative style of his music.

Check out: *The Rite of Spring,* which literally caused a riot at its premiere | *The Firebird,* which has one of the best finales anywhere in classical music | The *Symphony in C,* if you're feeling adventurous, is one that really grows on you.

Well, I Never! Stravinsky was a big friend of Rimsky-Korsakov (as well as being his pupil) and he wrote the music for R-K's wedding.

IGOR THEREFORE I AM

Igor Stravinsky was something of a rent-a-quote, having said some 'bon mot' about virtually every aspect of music at some point – a sort of Groucho Marx of classical music.

Here are a few of his rather cutting choice cuts:

Too many pieces of music finish too long after the end.

To listen is an effort, and just to hear is no merit. A duck hears also.

A good composer does not imitate; he steals.

I never understood the need for a 'live' audience. My music, because of its extreme quietude, would be happiest with a dead one.

On hearing John Cage's 4'33", which comprises no music,
just four and a half minutes of silence:
I look forward to hearing his longer works.

SERGEI PROKOFIEV (1891–1953)

This Russian composer suffered at the hands of Stalin, facing charges of composing music that worked against the State. Despite this, not only did he stay on in his homeland, he also left us with many great tunes. Some were influenced by the time he spent in America and Europe during the early part of his adult life.

Prokofiev's *Troika (Sleigh Ride)* comes in the middle of his *Lieutenant Kijé Suite*. When most people listen to it, they think of Christmas. Russians, however, would be forgiven for thinking 'drink'. It's a reworking of an old Russian drinking song.

When Prokofiev wrote his music to *Romeo and Juliet* in 1935, some critics thought he had gone too far in terms of poetic licence. He'd changed one of the most famous endings in all literature – and had made it happy! In the face of almost universal disapproval, he changed it back again to Shakespeare's classic finish.

Check out: *Peter and the Wolf* | the *Classical Symphony*, a sort of Prokofiev meets Mozart | *The Love for Three Oranges*, an opera, which has some great orchestral sections.

FOOTBALL SCORE

The Montagues and Capulets from Prokofiev's ballet *Romeo and Juliet* accompanies Sunderland footballers on to the pitch each week at home games.

CARL ORFF (1895–1982)

Carl Orff's *Carmina Burana* sniffed out the sweet smell of popularity after advertising executives decided that the opening '*O fortuna*' would be the perfect accompaniment to the crashing waves of an advertising campaign for Old Spice aftershave. And although it might sound all medieval and gothic (indeed, the words are quite saucy, in praise of wine, women and song), Orff died so recently that he may in fact have seen the Old Spice ad on the telly. Who knows? He himself may have splashed some on.

When *Carmina Burana* was first performed in 1937, it quickly became a hit. And Orff's reaction? He ordered his publisher to pulp every other work he had written up to that point.

Well, I Never! Orff was an expert in the music of Monteverdi, and edited an edition of his works.

TONIGHT, ON SOLO VACUUM CLEANER ...

What do composers do when they run out of conventional instruments for which they want to compose? Well, often they start to include all manner of weird and wonderful new 'instruments' in their scores. Gershwin put car horns in *An American in Paris,* Luciano Berio included a part for car springs, while the composer of silence, John Cage, once wrote a piece for liquidiser. And Malcolm Arnold really did write a piece for vacuum cleaner. Three vacuum cleaners in fact. Together with a floor polisher and four rifles.

GEORGE GERSHWIN (1898–1937)

Despite being written in the early part of the 20th century, Gershwin's music sounds very fresh and contemporary today. He was the master of fusing together jazz and classical music and was earning as much as $250,000 a year at the height of his popularity, which must make him one of the most financially successful of any composer in their own lifetime.

Check out: *Rhapsody in Blue* | *Piano Concerto* | His opera *Porgy and Bess* which includes the hit songs *'Summertime'* and *'I got Plenty o' Nuttin'* | *An American in Paris* – great musical pictures painted for orchestra.

Well, I Never! Gershwin wrote a song called *'I'm a poached egg!'* It's a love song, apparently, in which the singer compares his feelings of being without his loved one as being similar to a poached egg, separated from its toast.

THIRTY-SOMETHING COMPOSER DEATHS

There has always been a romantic image of the great composer as penniless, ill and dead by the age of 40. Is it true? Well, as for the last bit, there do seem to be a lot of composers who died in their thirties:

Schubert . . . . aged 31
Bellini . . . . aged 33
Mozart . . . . aged 35
Bizet . . . . aged 36
Purcell . . . . aged 36
Gershwin . . . . aged 38
Mendelssohn . . . . aged 38
Chopin . . . . aged 39
Weber . . . . aged 39

FINALES

Anton Webern is just one composer who met a rather sad, unfortunate end. He was shot by an American soldier after a misunderstanding that happened when he nipped outside to smoke a cigar during a curfew at the end of the Second World War. His contemporary, Alban Berg met his maker after being stung by a bee. Then there was Jean-Baptiste Lully, who hit himself in the toe with a conducting stick, and died from the wound after gangrene set in. And the list of strange composer deaths doesn't end there. The Spaniard, Enrique Granados drowned after the passenger cruise ship he was travelling on, was torpedoed by a German U-Boat during the First World War. The Russian, Alexander Borodin dropped dead in full national dress on the dance floor at a grand winter ball in St Petersburg, while the Frenchman Charles-Valentin Alkan was crushed to death by a bookcase, which fell on top of him. Alkan's fellow countryman, Ernest Chausson died after riding his bicycle into a brick wall. Compared to all that, Alexander Scriabin's death from a shaving cut seems, well, rather pedestrian.

$$\oint$$

KILLED IN ACTION

The life of the composer George Butterworth, best known for his quintessentially English piece *The Banks of Green Willow,* was tragically cut short when he was killed fighting for his country in the Battle of the Somme.

> *The whole problem can be stated quite simply by asking, 'Is there a meaning to music?' My answer to that would be, 'Yes'. And 'Can you state in so many words what the meaning is?' My answer to that would be, 'No'.*
> **AARON COPLAND, COMPOSER**

AARON COPLAND (1900–1990)

This American composer's best-known work, *Fanfare for the Common Man,* provides a stirring brassy opening to many public events in the USA. At their inauguration, presidents swear by it. Although Copland is thought of as being as American as apple pie, his parents were in fact both Russian and his original name was Kaplan.

Check out: The ballet suites *Rodeo* and *Appalachian Spring.*

Well, I Never! In the 1950s, Copland was hauled in front of the 'witch-hunt' committee of Joseph McCarthy, suspected of un-American activities. Copland gave as good as he got and was not asked to reappear.

> *Composers tend to assume that everyone loves music. Surprisingly enough, everyone doesn't.*
> **AARON COPLAND, COMPOSER**

JOAQUÍN RODRIGO (1901–1999)

The *Concierto de Aranjuez* is this Spanish composer's greatest hit outside his home country. It's also the most popular piece for guitar and orchestra, having been covered by so many people, from Miles Davis to the Grimethorpe Colliery Brass Band (as *Concerto de Orange Juice* in the film *Brassed Off!)*

Check out: *Fantasia para un Gentilhombre.*

Name drop: Paul Dukas, composer of *The Sorcerer's Apprentice*, who was Rodrigo's teacher.

GUITAR

The guitar in classical music is not quite the macho, trendy 'axe' of its rock music cousin. In fact, next to the full orchestra it has to fight to be heard, and is more often found in smaller groups or played solo. That's not to say there aren't some great guitar and orchestra pieces.

Check out: Rodrigo: *Concierto de Aranjuez* | Tarrega: *Recuerdos de La Alhambra* – both works which evoke warm Spanish countryside.

Name drop: Julian Bream | John Williams | Craig Ogden.

> *Artists who say they practise eight hours a day are liars or asses.*
> **ANDRÉS SEGOVIA, GUITARIST**

WILLIAM WALTON (1902–1983)

If Vaughan Williams' music can evoke a picture of pastoral England, then Walton is able to convey the majesty – the 'pomp' to Vaughan Williams' 'circumstance'. Pieces such as *Crown Imperial* and *Orb and Sceptre* seem to be written in the key of ermine.

Check out: *Spitfire Prelude and Fugue* | his *Henry V Suite,* written for Laurence Olivier's 1944 film.

VIOLA

Often the butt of jokes among professional musicians, the viola looks just like a violin, but is slightly bigger, makes a deeper sound and burns for longer when you set fire to it. That's the punch line to one of the jokes, by the way.

Check out: William Walton's *Viola Concerto*.

Name drop: Yuri Bashmet | Julian Rachlin.

A FURTHER SELECTION OF VIOLA JOKES

How do you prevent your violin from being stolen?
Put it in a viola case.

What's the difference between a viola and a trampoline?
You take your shoes off to jump on a trampoline.

How is lightning like a viola player's fingers?
Neither one strikes in the same place twice.

Why do viola players stand for long periods outside people's houses?
They can't find the key and they don't know when to come in.

What's the difference between a viola and an onion?
Nobody cries when you cut up a viola.

ARAM KHACHATURIAN (1903–1978)

Two pieces of music written for separate ballets top the list of this Armenian composer's most played work. The *Sabre Dance* from *Gayaneh* may have made him famous around the globe just after it was written in the 1940s, but for a whole generation he will always be the man behind the theme tune to *The Onedin Line*. This piece's real name is the *Adagio of Spartacus and Phrygia*.

Check out: The *Galop* and the *Waltz* from *Masquerade Suite*.

Well, I Never! Khachaturian's first instrument was a tuba.

DMITRI SHOSTAKOVICH (1906–1975)

Among the greatest of 20th century composers, Shostakovich spent his entire life falling in and out of favour with the ruling Communist Party in Russia. Despite the pressure over what sort of music he should compose, he still managed to write a stack of hits. He was also one of the first great film composers – with many of his movie scores still being performed today.

Check out: *Jazz Suites Nos. 1* and *2* | *Romance* from *The Gadfly* | *The Assault on Beautiful Gorky* | *Symphony No. 5* | *Piano Concerto No. 2*.

Well, I Never! Having come in for some stick with his previous works, Shostakovich subtitled his *Fifth Symphony* 'A Soviet Artist's Response to Just Criticism' and people have been arguing over what he meant ever since.

Music with dinner is an insult both to the cook and the violinist.
G.K. CHESTERTON, WRITER

OUT OF THIS WORLD

The first cosmonaut, Yuri Gagarin, sang a song called *My Homeland Hears,* written by the great Russian composer Dmitri Shostakovich, over the radio link from his spacecraft back to earth.

THE BORROWERS

Over the years, many great composers have included popular songs in their music. For example, Shostakovich's Jazz Suites contain *Tea for Two,* Saint-Saëns borrowed the *Can-Can,* played very slowly to represent the tortoise in the *Carnival of the Animals,* and Walton's *Façade* contains '*Oh, I do like to be beside the seaside*'.

The converse is also true, with many classical music pieces gaining chart success by being made into pop songs. They include '*Since Yesterday*' by Strawberry Switchblade (Sibelius's *Fifth Symphony*), '*Nut Rocker*' by Bee Bumble and the Stingers (Tchaikovsky's *Nutcracker),* and '*Altogether Now*' by The Farm (Pachelbel's *Canon in D).*

IDENTITY THEFT

It's not just tunes that pop singers have borrowed from classical music. The 1970s crooner, Gerry Dorsey, pinched his stage name from the German composer, Engelbert Humperdink. Born in 1854, his opera *Hänsel and Gretel* remains his most enduring work. But Engelbert Humperdink – the pop singer – is more famous for his chart hits '*Release Me*' and '*The Last Waltz*'.

SAMUEL BARBER (1910–1981)

One of the most popular American composers, Samuel Barber is best known for his *Adagio for Strings,* which was used to great effect by the director Oliver Stone in his Vietnam War movie, *Platoon.* More recently, his hauntingly beautiful *Violin Concerto,* composed on the death of his mother, has become a firm Classic FM favourite. Barber's *Symphony No. 2* was commissioned by the U.S. Army Air Forces in 1944. It included an electronic instrument, which imitated the sound of the radio signals used for air navigation. When he revised the work in 1947, he replaced the instrument with an E-flat clarinet.

Not to be confused with: *The Barber of Seville,* which is an opera by Rossini | Babar the Elephant, which is a piece for voice and piano (or orchestra) by Poulenc.

Name drop: Toscanini, the conductor, whose idea it was to re-orchestrate the slow movement of his String Quartet. This became what is often now called *'the Barber Adagio'.*

Even the delights of the Moonlight Sonata *couldn't draw Reginald's gaze from Clarissa's dandruff.*

143

BENJAMIN BRITTEN (1913–1976)

This composer has possibly the most appropriate sounding surname ever, as he seems to stand for everything that symbolised Britain in the mid-20th century. For much of his life he lived in Aldeburgh, on the Suffolk coast, where he founded the music festival that still continues every year, in June. He is buried in Aldeburgh church, beside his partner, the tenor Peter Pears. In 1976, he was made a Life Peer – the very first composer in Britain ever to receive the honour.

Check out: for a great introduction to Britten, try something like the *Sea Interludes* from *Peter Grimes* or the *Ceremony of Carols* | If you'd like to delve a little deeper, try the *Serenade for tenor, horn and strings*, written for Pears.

Well, I Never! Britten was a conscientious objector during the Second World War. He was excused military service in exchange for his participation in official state music-making.

> *Composing is like driving down a foggy road toward a house. Slowly, you see more details of the house – the colour of the slates and bricks, the shape of the windows. The notes are the bricks and mortar of the house.*
> **BENJAMIN BRITTEN, COMPOSER**

> *The old idea ... of a composer suddenly having a terrific idea and sitting up all night to write it is nonsense. Night time is for sleeping.*
> **BENJAMIN BRITTEN, COMPOSER**

FAMOUS OPERAS: WHAT IS ACTUALLY GOING ON?

NO. 10: BRITTEN: *PETER GRIMES* (OR *LITTLE BRITTEN*)

Britten's Peter Grimes is both very modern and a real classic. It deals with Britten's favourite theme of the outsider in a small community. Interspersed throughout the opera are the gorgeous *Sea Interludes* which are much loved by Classic FM's listeners.

⊙ THE PLOT ⊙

The Prologue

We're in the parish hall of an East Coast fishing village, in around 1830. The opera opens on an inquest into the death, at sea, of Peter Grimes's apprentice. The villagers suspect Grimes, but he explains that the wind blew them off course for three days and the boy died of exposure. The coroner believes Grimes but tells him he should not take another boy out – he should find himself a grown up. No one really wants to hear Grimes's version of events, but he does find some sort of kindred spirit in Ellen Orford, the schoolteacher. That's the end of the prologue.

Act 1

We are down by the boats. Ned Keene tells Peter he has found him another boy apprentice, who just needs fetching from the workhouse. The villagers refuse to have anything to do with the whole affair, but Ellen speaks up for Peter. Someone spies a storm at sea and they all hope that the sea will not be too cruel. A local captain, Balstrode, tells Grimes he's best off leaving the gossip of the village behind, but Peter says his roots are here. He tells Balstrode of the days at sea, with only the apprentice's corpse for company. He also muses how lovely life would be if Ellen were to become his wife. Gosh, he doesn't waste time, does he? In the warm and cosy pub that night, all local life is there: the old lady, waiting for her laudanum from the chemist; the drunk, Bob Boles, making unwanted advances towards her nieces. Each time the door opens, the elements burst in.

When Peter arrives, things get a little tense. Ned Keene gets everyone doing some community singing, to distract them. Hobson and the new apprentice arrive and Peter leads him off home. The crowd all say 'Home? You call that home?' End of Act 1 – time for a tub of cockles and vinegar.

Act 2

It's a Sunday morning. Ellen is talking to John, Peter's new apprentice, about the relative merits of the workhouse over teaching. Or is it the other way round? She's worried to find his coat torn and his neck bruised. Peter comes in to take the boy off to work, despite it being a Sunday. Ellen and Peter quarrel, and he storms off with the boy, leaving Ellen to go home crying. When the congregation come out of the nearby church, some have heard the quarrelling and put two and two together. They ask Ellen to say what happened and get the impression that Peter is intent on murder. The men march off to Peter's beach hut. Before they get there, we see Peter in the hut with his new apprentice. He's still going on about how great life would have been if he'd been with Ellen. Then he hears the crowd approaching. He presumes they're coming to get the boy, and tries to hide him, bundling him down the cliff. The boy falls to his death with a bloodcurdling scream, and Peter climbs down after him. To lose one apprentice is unfortunate, but to lose two is careless. End of Act 2 - crabsticks with thousand island dressing.

Act 3

There's a dance in the village hall. All the usual suspects are there. One of them tries to enlist support for the notion of going after Peter Grimes and charging him with murder. Ellen and Balstrode discuss the fact that Peter is nowhere to be seen. They have, however, found John the apprentice's yellow jersey washed up on the beach. Ah! Balstrode still thinks they might be able to help Peter.

Meanwhile, a posse of baying locals are gathered together to find Grimes. The search party can be heard shouting his name around the place, interspersed with the sound of the foghorn. Grimes is there, madly rambling on about home and all that has happened. Ellen and Balstrode find him and tell him they've come to take him home. Peter, ever so slightly wobbly, continues to ramble. Balstrode decides there's nothing they can do and tells him to take his boat out to sea and sink it. He comforts Ellen and leads her off.

Next morning in the village, the coastguard's report says that a boat has been seen out at sea, sinking. No one is particularly bothered. They carry on with their day.

COMPOSERS WHO SHARE BIRTHDAYS

Bruch and Scriabin .... (Jan 6th)

Palestrina and Mendelssohn .... (Feb 3rd)

Smetana and Vivaldi .... (March 4th)

Telemann and Johann Strauss Sr .... (March 14th)

Bach and Mussorgsky .... (March 21st)

Busoni and Rachmaninov .... (April 1st)

Brahms and Tchaikovsky .... (April 7th)

Massenet and Fauré .... (April 12th)

Albinoni and Schumann .... (June 8th)

Gounod and Stravinsky .... (June 17th)

Pachelbel and Humperdinck .... (September 1st)

Bruckner and Milhaud .... (September 4th)

Boyce and Arvo Pärt .... (September 11th)

Shostakovich and Rameau .... (September 25th)

Saint-Saëns and Verdi .... (October 9th)

Johann Strauss Jr and Bizet .... (October 25th)

Hummel and Copland .... (November 14th)

Rodrigo and Britten .... (November 22nd)

$\oint$

LEONARD BERNSTEIN (1918–1990)

This American composer's biggest hit was the musical *West Side Story*. Bernstein wrote the music and Stephen Sondheim wrote the words – what a partnership! He also spent a lot of his life touring as a very successful conductor.

Check out: His overture to *Candide* and see if you can stop your foot from tapping | *Chichester Psalms*, beautiful music written to a commission from the Dean of Chichester in the 1960s.

Well, I Never! Bernstein sometimes composed music under the pseudonym of 'Lenny Amber'. And how did he arrive at this pen name? Well, in German, the word for 'amber' is 'Bernstein'.

147

POETIC LICENCE

Leonard Bernstein was a Professor at the renowned American university, Harvard. You might have expected him to have held the role in the field of music. Instead, he was actually a Professor of Poetry, which was another art form in which he dabbled. Six of the lectures he gave in 1973, while he was in the position, are still available on DVD today.

MUSICAL MEANING

The word 'philharmonic' is liberally sprinkled throughout the names of many of the world's greatest orchestras. In the UK we have the Royal Philharmonic Orchestra, the Royal Liverpool Philharmonic Orchestra, the London Philharmonic Orchestra and even the Philharmonia Orchestra. But what does the word actually mean? It comes from the two Greek words *phileo* and *harmonikos*. When they're welded together 'philharmonic' translates as 'harmony loving'.

SIR MALCOLM ARNOLD (1921–2006)

Arnold gave up his job as principal trumpet in the London Philharmonic Orchestra, to become a composer full-time. He became particularly well-known for his work for the cinema and won an Oscar for his soundtrack to *The Bridge on the River Kwai*.

Check out: *Eight English Dances* | *Four Scottish Dances* | *Four Cornish Dances*.

TRUMPET

This is the best-known member of the brass family, with a long history stretching back to biblical times. It is more agile than the trombone because it has three buttons (valves) instead of a slide. Its ability to be heard over a church organ has made it very popular at weddings.

Check out: Hummel: *Trumpet Concerto* | John Stanley: *Trumpet Voluntary in D* | Haydn: *Trumpet Concerto* | Armenian composer Arutunian's *Trumpet Concerto*, an absolute staple of the trumpet player's repertoire.

Name drop: John Wallace | Wynton Marsalis | Hakan Hadenberger | Alison Balsom.

> **"** *There's only two ways to sum up music: either it's good or it's bad. If it's good you don't mess about it – you just enjoy it.* **"**
> **LOUIS ARMSTRONG, TRUMPET PLAYER**

WHEREFORE ART THOU ...

These composers have all written music based on William Shakespeare's play *Romeo and Juliet*:

Armstrong
Bellini
Berlioz
Bernstein
Delius
Gounod
Prokofiev
Tchaikovsky

149

HENRYK GÓRECKI (BORN 1933)

This Polish composer shot to fame back in 1992 when Classic FM started to play a recording of his *Symphony No. 3* featuring the soprano Dawn Upshaw with the London Sinfonietta. The heart-rending second movement of this work, which has the subtitle *Symphony of Sorrowful Songs,* is a setting of a prayer found scratched into a cell wall of the Nazi Gestapo's headquarters, written by a young girl in the Second World War.

None of his other music has come anywhere close to repeating his second symphony's success. And don't let the name catch you out – even though it doesn't look like it, it's pronounced 'Goretski'.

Check out: *Totus Tuus*, a haunting and striking hymn to the Virgin Mary.

PETER MAXWELL DAVIES (BORN 1934)

The current Master of the Queen's Music has had a long career composing critically acclaimed works. He is the founder of the St. Magnus Festival in Orkney, the Scottish islands where he has lived since 1971. *The Manchester Group* is the name of the group of composers and musicians in which he first came to prominence, and includes fellow modernist Sir Harrison Birtwistle.

Check out: *Farewell to Stromness,* a solo piano piece performed by the composer, has captured the imagination of Classic FM listeners. It was written as a protest against a nuclear reprocessing plant on one of the Orkney isles.

Name drop: Everyone who knows him refers to Sir Peter simply as 'Max'.

*Music hath charms to soothe the savage
beast, but I'd try a revolver first.*
JOHN BILLINGS, HUMORIST

ARVO PÄRT (BORN 1935)

This Estonian composer sits alongside John Tavener, Henryk Górecki and John Rutter as one of the most popular modern choral writers. His laid-back, gentle sound is the musical equivalent of an empty, white room and appeals to 'chillout' enthusiasts just as much as to classical fans. To pronounce his name correctly, imagine a 'pear' than add a soft 't'. Pärt gives the impression of being a composer who is striving to write the perfect piece. Some would say he already has.

Check out: *Spiegel im Spiegel* | If you're feeling more adventurous, try the *Cantus in Memoriam Benjamin Britten*, or *Tabula Rasa*.

COMPOSERS BORN ON SIGNIFICANT DAYS

April Fool's Day . . . . Rachmaninov
US Independence Day . . . . Daquin
St. David's Day . . . . Chopin
Christmas Day . . . . Gibbons
Leap Year Day . . . . Rossini
Bastille Day . . . . Finzi
St. Andrew's Day . . . . Alkan

PHILIP GLASS (BORN 1937)

Arguably one of the most respected living American composers, Glass's music receives its widest audience through his film soundtracks. He belongs to the group of composers known as 'minimalists', whose music is made up of simple rhythms, repeated over and over again.

Check out: *Violin Concerto | Koyaanisqatsi | Kundun | The Hours.*

JON LORD (BORN 1941)

Perhaps most famous as a member of the rock group *Deep Purple,* Lord is one of a number of musicians who have flexed their classical credentials over the past few years. His purely classical *Durham Concerto* was the highest new entry in the Classic FM Hall of Fame in 2009, but Lord has been combining rock and classical music for three decades, with his *Concerto for Group and Orchestra* receiving its debut at London's Royal Albert Hall back in 1969. One of the genuinely nice guys of the composing world, Lord also has the finest pony-tail among any of the living composers featured in this book.

Check out: *Boom of the Tingling Strings* – a piano concerto.

Well, I Never! In one movement of *The Durham Concerto,* Lord quotes the old tune *Gaudeamus Igitur,* just as Brahms had done in his *Academic Festival Overture.* The effect is just as thrilling.

> **About a soprano:**
> *If she can strike a low G or F like a death-rattle and high F like the shriek of a little dog when you step on its tail, the house will resound with acclamations.*
> **HECTOR BERLIOZ, COMPOSER**

PAUL McCARTNEY (BORN 1942)

Although Sir Paul McCartney's best-known compositions were co-written with John Lennon in the 60s, a few years ago he carved out a new career for himself by turning his hand to classical music. His classical works have proved that his knack for writing a strong, catchy melody has not deserted him.

In fact, the Fab Four's links to classical music go back a long way – Beethoven's ninth symphony and part of Wagner's *Lohengrin* both feature in the Beatles' movie *Help*.

Check out: *Liverpool Oratorio | The Leaf | Standing Stone | Working Classical | Ecce Cor Meum | A Garland for Linda*, a collection of ten pieces for his late wife by various composers, for which McCartney himself wrote *Nova*.

Name drop: John Rutter, who also contributed a piece to *A Garland for Linda*, and is a big Beatles fan.

MICHAEL NYMAN (BORN 1941)

This minimalist British composer has written many film soundtracks, the best known of which is *The Piano*. He later turned the score into a single movement *Piano Concerto*.

In Jane Campion's 1992 film, Holly Hunter was cast as a piano teacher. Hunter, a pianist herself, learnt to play Nyman's solo piano music in order that she might actually play the piano on set. So, to sum up, Holly Hunter, who plays the piano, plays the piano in *The Piano*. Glad we cleared that one up.

Well, I Never! Nyman is widely credited with applying the term 'minimalism' to music around 1970. Before then, it was the preserve of the visual arts.

JOHN TAVENER (BORN 1944)

John Tavener's music reached its biggest-ever audience when his *Song for Athene* was used at the end of the funeral service held at Westminster Abbey for Diana, Princess of Wales. In the 1980s he wrote *The Protecting Veil* for the cellist Steven Isserlis and more recently found his choral piece *The Lamb* being used on TV to sell mobile phones.

Not to be confused with: John Taverner, with two 'r's, an English composer of sacred music born some 450 years earlier than John Tavener, with one 'r'.

> *I am sitting in the smallest room of my house. I have your review before me. In a moment, it will be behind me.*
> **COMPOSER MAX REGER, IN A LETTER TO A MUSIC CRITIC**

KARL JENKINS (BORN 1944)

Karl Jenkins has had a varied career, ranging from being principal oboist in the National Youth Orchestra of Wales to being a leading member of the seventies' rock outfit Soft Machine. *Adiemus: Songs of Sanctuary* was an instant hit with Classic FM listeners back in 1995 and, like much of Jenkins' music, has become even more famous through being used in TV advertising campaigns. More recently, *The Armed Man: A Mass for Peace* has achieved a kind of cult status with listeners, with the *Benedictus* becoming particularly popular.

Check out: *Palladio* | *Requiem* | *Stabat Mater*.

Well, I Never! Karl's recording studio in central London is called Moustache Studios, a reference to his Elgar-like, handlebar lip cover.

JOHN RUTTER (BORN 1945)

John Rutter's music is probably performed more often and in more places around Britain than any other living British classical composer. Based in Cambridge, his choral anthems and carols have become a major part of church services in this country. His most famous works are his small anthems, such as *For the Beauty of the Earth* and *The Lord Bless You and Keep You*. His stunningly beautiful *Requiem* is often performed by amateur choral groups.

Check out: *A Gaelic Blessing,* often referred to by mischievous choirboys as '*A Garlic Dressing*' | *A Clare Benediction* | *The Candlelight Carol.*

> *[Music] can be made anywhere,*
> *is invisible, and does not smell.*
> **W. H. AUDEN, POET, *IN PRAISE***
> ***OF LIMESTONE* (1951)**

I CAN'T BELIEVE IT'S NOT...

John Rutter is a real British success story and should be celebrated as such. His music is particularly popular in America and he has also penned a large number of Christmas carols, making him a firm fixture during most festive choral concerts. Such is his music's ubiquity, that whenever some choristers are asked to sing a carol by another living composer, they are rumoured to remark: 'I can't believe it's not Rutter!' in homage to the well known brand of low fat spread.

JAY UNGAR (BORN 1946)

This American composer became a star when a superb arrangement of his tune *The Ashokan Farewell* was played on Classic FM. There was a huge response from listeners to the piece, which was used as the theme to a television documentary called *The American Civil War*. It has now rocketed into the Top 20 of the annual Classic FM Hall of Fame listener vote in an arrangement by the former Royal Marine musician, Major J.R. Perkins. So far, Ungar resolutely remains a one-hit-wonder. It is of no relevance, whatsoever, that he shares his surname with the character played by Jack Lemmon in *The Odd Couple*.

I cannot tell you how much I love to play for people. Would you believe it – sometimes when I sit down to practise and there is no one else in the room, I have to stifle an impulse to ring for the elevator man and offer him money to come and hear me.
ARTUR RUBINSTEIN, PIANIST

BOGEY AT THE 18TH

It's said that Kenneth J. Alford got the idea for the tune *Colonel Bogey* while on the golf course. When his golf partner teed off, he would always whistle two notes to warn anyone on the fairway. The notes stuck in his head, all the way round, and became the first two notes of the now world famous tune.

COMPOSERS' STAR SIGNS

Aquarius
Delius, Mendelssohn, Mozart

Pisces
Barber, Chopin, Delibes, Handel, Rimsky-Korsakov

Aries
J.S. Bach, Bartók, Haydn, Rachmaninov

Taurus
Brahms, Fauré, Prokofiev, Tchaikovsky

Gemini
Elgar, Grieg, Offenbach, Wagner

Cancer
Gluck, Mahler, Orff

Leo
Debussy, Glazunov

Virgo
Bruckner, Dvořák, Holst, Pachelbel

Libra
Gershwin, Saint-Saëns, Shostakovich, Vaughan Williams

Scorpio
Bizet, Borodin, Britten, Copland, J. Strauss Jr

Sagittarius
Beethoven, Berlioz, Donizetti, de Falla

Capricorn
Bruch, Poulenc, Puccini

ZBIGNIEW PREISNER (BORN 1955)

When the *Requiem for my Friend* was released in 1996, it became an instant hit with Classic FM listeners. The friend in the title is the Polish film director Krzystof Kieslowski, he of the *Three Colours* trilogy fame, for whose movies Preisner had written the music.

Check out: *La Double Vie de Véronique* (soundtrack) – cult movie with inherited cult status for its music.

> *Definition of a true musician: one who, when he hears a lady singing in the bathtub, puts his ear to the keyhole.*
> **MOREY AMSTERDAM, ACTOR AND COMEDIAN**

LUDOVICO EINAUDI (BORN 1955)

This Italian pianist and composer is now a firm favourite with Classic FM listeners. He has become known particularly for his beautifully haunting melodies for solo piano.

Check out: *Stanze | Le Onde | Eden Roc | I Giorni | Una Mattina.*

> *Learning music by reading about it is like making love by mail.*
> **ISAAC STERN, VIOLINIST**

> *Mine was the kind of piece in which nobody knew what was going on – including the composer, the conductor and the critics. Consequently I got pretty good critics.*
> **OSCAR LEVANT, PIANIST AND COMPOSER,**
> *A SMATTERING OF IGNORANCE* **(1940)**

HOWARD GOODALL (BORN 1958)

If you've ever watched *Blackadder, Mr Bean, Red Dwarf, The Catherine Tate Show, Q.I.* or *The Vicar of Dibley*, then you will already know Howard Goodall's music. Among the most successful television theme tune writers of all time, Howard has also composed musicals and film soundtracks. He is well-known for his choral music and as Classic FM's third Composer-in-Residence, he wrote *Enchanted Voices*, an album based on the Beatitudes, which stormed to the top of the Specialist Classical Chart upon its release and stayed there for months. He was named Composer of the Year at the Classical Brit Awards in 2009, following the release of *Eternal Light: A Requiem*, which was incorporated into a ballet by the Rambert Dance Company. As well as presenting a weekly programme on Classic FM, he has become a regular face on television, presenting programmes such as *Howard Goodall's Big Bangs* and *How Music Works* for Channel 4. Goodall is also a passionate advocate for the benefits of music education and is England's first National Singing Ambassador.

Check out: *Ecce Homo* (the theme to *Mr Bean*) | *Psalm 23* (the theme to *The Vicar of Dibley*) | *The Seasons*.

Well, I Never! Howard Goodall was a contemporary at Oxford University of the actor Rowan Atkinson and the film writer-producer Richard Curtis. The three have continued to work together regularly throughout their careers.

PATRICK HAWES (BORN 1958)

Classic FM's second Composer-in-Residence, Hawes made his name with the album *Blue in Blue*, which featured the beautiful choral piece *Quanta Qualia*. His collection of solo piano works which were written during his time as Classic FM's Composer-in-Residence are gathered together on the album *Towards the Light*. Although his particular interest is in music written in the Renaissance and Baroque periods, his own personal sound owes more to the English Romantic tradition of Delius and Vaughan Williams.

Check out: *Song of Songs,* a work for voices and orchestra.

SELECTED CONTEMPORARY WORKS
CHAMPIONED BY CLASSIC FM

These works have become synonymous with Classic FM since the station's launch in 1992:

Karl Jenkins: *Adiemus: Songs of Sanctuary*
Jay Ungar (arranged Perkins): *The Ashokan Farewell*
Henryk Górecki: *Symphony No. 3 (Symphony of Sorrowful Songs)*
Ludovico Einaudi: *Le Onde*
Peter Maxwell Davies: *Farewell to Stromness*
Nigel Hess: *Ladies in Lavender*
John Brunning: *Pie Jesu*
Howard Goodall: *Pro Alios Curantibus*
Jon Lord: *Durham Concerto*
Patrick Hawes: *Quanta Qualia*
Paul McCartney: *Standing Stone*
Patrick Doyle: *My Father's Favourite*

10 KIDS' CLASSICS

Bartók – *For Children*
Bizet: *Jeux d'enfants*
Brahms – *Lullaby*
Britten – *The Young Person's Guide to the Orchestra*
Debussy – *Children's Corner*
Fauré – *Dolly Suite*
Mozart, L. – *Toy Symphony*
Poulenc – *The Story of Babar, the Little Elephant*
Prokofiev – *Peter and the Wolf*
Saint-Saëns – *Carnival of the Animals*

JOBY TALBOT (BORN 1971)

Joby Talbot was named as Classic FM's first ever Composer-in-Residence in a scheme supported by the PRS Foundation for the promotion of new music. He has composed a wide range of classical, pop and film music. He first came to prominence as a member of the pop group *The Divine Comedy*.

Check out: *The Dying Swan* | *Robbie the Reindeer* | *The League of Gentlemen* | *The Hitchhiker's Guide to the Galaxy*.

> *I occasionally play works by*
> *contemporary composers, and for two reasons.*
> *First, to discourage the composer from writing any*
> *more, and secondly to remind myself how*
> *much I appreciate Beethoven.*
> **JASCHA HEIFETZ, VIOLINIST**

CHRISTMAS MUSIC

The tunes of some of the best-loved carols were, in fact, written by classical music greats (*Hark the Herald* by Mendelssohn, *In the Bleak Midwinter* by Holst). As well as the hymns we sing each year, there's also a festive sack-load of longer pieces, such as the *Carol Symphony* by the exquisitely named Victor Hely-Hutchinson, or the *Christmas Overture* by Nigel Hess, which are perfect for having on in the background as the family arrive on Christmas Eve.

THE UK'S FAVOURITE CHRISTMAS CAROLS

Every year, we ask our listeners to pick their favourite Christmas carols. These are the results of the poll from Christmas 2008:

In the Bleak Midwinter
O Little Town of Bethlehem
Silent Night
Hark! The Herald Angels Sing
O Holy Night
O come, O come Emmanuel
Coventry Carol
In dulci jubilo
O come, all ye faithful
It came upon the midnight clear
The First Nowell
Past three o'clock
God rest ye Merry, Gentlemen
Gabriel's message
Once in Royal David's City
Gaudete
Star Carol
Away in a manger
Tomorrow shall be my dancing day
Angels from the realms of Glory
Sussex Carol

Good King Wenceslas
The Little Road to Bethlehem
Ding Dong merrily on high
The Holly and the Ivy
See amid the winter's snow
Shepherd's Pipe Carol
I saw three ships
Cherry Tree Carol
Angel's Carol
While Shepherds watched their flocks by night
Nativity Carol
We wish you a Merry Christmas
Rocking Carol
Unto us is born a son
Deck the hills with boughs of holly
Donkey Carol
Birthday Carol
Sans Day Carol
Candlelight Carol

SUMMER SNOW

Leroy Anderson's *Sleigh Ride* is a perennial Christmas favourite, but if you thought that he composed it in the deep midwinter, then you would be wrong. The musical score comes complete with a hose whip and was actually written during the height of a summer heat wave.

About contemporary music:
Three farts and a raspberry, orchestrated.
SIR JOHN BARBIROLLI, CONDUCTOR

FILM MUSIC

There's a long history of music being used in films, right back to the days when a pianist would accompany silent movies with a live performance. Many of the greatest pieces of classical music by composers as varied as Mozart, Beethoven and Wagner have cinematic heritage. Add to this a long tradition of composers being commissioned to write music especially for the cinema and we're talking quite a large section in the record shop. Copland, Vaughan Williams, Walton, Prokofiev and Shostakovich all have soundtracks to their names. More recently, Howard Shore, John Barry, James Horner and Hans Zimmer have all given the undoubted king of movie composers, John Williams, a run for his money. The first ever dedicated soundtrack was composed by Saint-Saëns for the 1908 film *L'assassinat du Duc de Guise*.

BIG SCREEN CONTROVERSY

The film director Ken Russell has specialised in making movies about the lives of many of the great composers. Often highly controversial and containing scenes which are very definitely of an adult nature, Russell's classical music films have included:

Elgar (1962)
The Debussy Film (1965)
Song of Summer (1968 – about Delius)
Dance of the Seven Veils (1970 – about Richard Strauss)
The Music Lovers (1970 – about Tchaikovsky)
Mahler (1974)
Lisztomania (1975)
The Secret Life of Arnold Bax (1992)

JOHN WILLIAMS (BORN 1932)

Arguably the greatest living film composer. If a movie has a John Williams soundtrack, it nearly always means that it's a Hollywood blockbuster. His hit list includes *Star Wars, Harry Potter, Schindler's List, Superman* and *E.T.*

Not to be confused with: the other John Williams, a brilliant classical guitarist.

Name drop: The London Symphony Orchestra, with whom Williams has a long term relationship. They have recorded many of his soundtracks, including *Raiders of the Lost Ark, Superman* and all of the *Star Wars* movies.

JOHN BARRY (BORN 1933)

British composer who made his name with his music for films. More recently he has had a number of big hits with his CDs of orchestral music. His style is very lush, almost epic, and he has a talent for very hummable tunes.

Check out: *The Beyondness of Things | Dances with Wolves.*

HOWARD SHORE (BORN 1946)

This Canadian film composer has soared in popularity following the release of his soundtrack to the film version of *The Lord of the Rings* in 2001. He has also written the music to the two sequels.

Check out: *Gangs of New York | The Aviator | Panic Room.*

Well, I Never! Shore was in the house-band of cult American comedy television series *Saturday Night Live*. The show also featured Dan Ackroyd and John Belushi, who went on to star in *The Blues Brothers*. Shore is widely credited with coming up with the name for the band, which went on to become the basis of the wildly popular movie.

CELLULOID SUCCESS

In 1978, the London Symphony Orchestra won three Grammy Awards for its performance of the soundtrack to the original *Star Wars* movie. The orchestra has played on every *Star Wars* film since. The LSO is not above a little screen stardom of its own either, having appeared in cartoon form on both *The Simpsons* and *Family Guy*.

CLASSICAL MUSIC USED IN FILMS

ACE VENTURA PET
DETECTIVE
Mozart: *Eine kleine Nachtmusik*

AN AMERICAN WEREWOLF
IN LONDON
Ravel: *Daphnis and Chloé*

APOCALYPSE NOW
Wagner: *Ride of the Valkyries*

AS GOOD AS IT GETS
Gershwin: *An American in Paris*

BABE
Saint-Saëns: *Symphony No. 3*

A BEAUTIFUL MIND
Mozart: *Piano Sonata No. 11*

BEND IT LIKE BECKHAM
Puccini: '*Nessun Dorma*' from
Turandot

BILLY ELLIOTT
Tchaikovsky: *Swan Lake*

BRASSED OFF!
Rodrigo: *Concierto de Aranjuez*

BRIDGET JONES'S DIARY
Handel: *Hallelujah Chorus* from
Messiah

CAPTAIN CORELLI'S
MANDOLIN
Puccini: '*O mio babbino caro*'
from *Gianni Schicchi*

CATCH ME IF YOU CAN
Haydn: *Piano Concerto No. 11*

CHARIOTS OF FIRE
Allegri: *Miserere*

A CLOCKWORK ORANGE
Beethoven: *Symphony No. 9*

DEAD POETS SOCIETY
Beethoven: *Piano Concerto No. 5*

DIE HARD
Bach: *Brandenburg Concerto No. 3*

DRIVING MISS DAISY
Dvořák: *Song to the Moon*
from *Rusalka*

THE ELEPHANT MAN
Barber: *Adagio for Strings*

THE ENGLISH PATIENT
Bach: *Aria* from *Goldberg
Variations*

FOUR WEDDINGS AND
A FUNERAL
Handel: *Arrival of the Queen
of Sheba*

THE FRENCH LIEUTENANT'S
WOMAN
Mozart: *Piano Sonata No. 15*

THE HORSE WHISPERER
Beethoven: *Cello Sonata No. 1*

INDECENT PROPOSAL
Vivaldi: *Concerto No. 8* from
L'Estro Armonico

JFK
Mozart: *Horn Concerto No. 2*

JOHNNY ENGLISH
Handel: *Zadok the Priest*

L.A. CONFIDENTIAL
Mendelssohn: *Hebrides Overture*

THE LADYKILLERS
Boccherini: *Minuet*

LARA CROFT TOMB RAIDER
Bach: *Keyboard Concerto No. 5
in F minor*

MONA LISA
Puccini: *Love Duet* from
Madame Butterfly

MR. HOLLAND'S OPUS
Beethoven: *Symphony No. 7*

MRS. DOUBTFIRE
Rossini: '*Largo al factotum*' from
The Barber of Seville

MY BIG FAT GREEK
WEDDING
Wagner: *Bridal Chorus* from
Lohengrin

MY LEFT FOOT
Schubert: *Trout Quintet*

NATURAL BORN KILLERS
Orff: *Carmina Burana*

OCEAN'S ELEVEN
Debussy: *Clair de lune*

OUT OF AFRICA
Mozart: *Clarinet Concerto*

PHILADELPHIA
Mozart: *Laudate Dominum*

PLATOON
Barber: *Adagio for Strings*

PRETTY WOMAN
Vivaldi: *Four Seasons*

A ROOM WITH A VIEW
Puccini: *Doretta's Dream* from
La Rondine

THE SHAWSHANK
REDEMPTION
Mozart: '*Che soave zeffiretto*'
from *The Marriage of Figaro*

THE SILENCE OF THE LAMBS
Bach: *Goldberg Variations*

SLEEPING WITH THE ENEMY
Berlioz: *Symphonie Fantastique*

THE TALENTED MR. RIPLEY
Bach: *Italian Concerto*

THERE IS SOMETHING
ABOUT MARY
Bizet: *Danse behémienne* from
Carmen Suite No. 2

TOY STORY 2
R. Strauss: *Also sprach
Zarathustra*

TRAINSPOTTING
Bizet: *Habanera* from *Carmen*

THE TRUMAN SHOW
Chopin: *Piano Concerto No. 1*

WALL STREET
Verdi: '*Questa, o quella*' from
Rigoletto

WAYNE'S WORLD
Tchaikovsky: *Romeo and Juliet*

WHO FRAMED ROGER
RABBIT
Liszt: *Hungarian Rhapsody No. 2*

20,000 LEAGUES UNDER THE
SEA
Bach: *Toccata and Fugue in D
minor*

2001: A SPACE ODYSSEY
R. Strauss: *Also sprach
Zarathustra*

JAMES HORNER (BORN 1953)

One of the most commercially successful film composers, James Horner has scored more than a hundred films. He has won three Grammy Awards, two Academy Awards and has a further five Oscar nominations and four Golden Globe nominations. He is far and away best known for his score to *Titanic*.

Check out: *Apollo 13* | *Braveheart* | *Field of Dreams* | *A Beautiful Mind* | *The Perfect Storm* | *The Missing* | *The Mask of Zorro* | *Iris*.

Name drop: *Spectral Shimmers*, one of the few pieces of non-film music Horner has written. It was premiered by the Indianapolis Symphony Orchestra.

PATRICK DOYLE (BORN 1953)

Almost certainly the most successful Scottish contemporary film composer, Patrick Doyle studied at the Royal Scottish Academy of Music and Drama in Glasgow. His film soundtracks range from *Henry V* and *Much Ado About Nothing* through to *Bridget Jones's Diary*, *Killing Me Softly*, *Gosford Park* and *Calendar Girls*. His 1995 soundtrack to *Sense and Sensibility* is his greatest critical success, earning him award nominations from the Golden Globes, the Oscars and the BAFTAs. His ascent into the very top flight of international film soundtrack composers was confirmed when he was asked to take over the *Harry Potter* franchise from John Williams, as the composer of the soundtrack to *Harry Potter and the Goblet of Fire*.

Check out: the beautifully relaxing *My Father's Favourite* from the soundtrack to *Sense and Sensibility*.

NIGEL HESS (BORN 1953)

Notable as a film and television composer, Hess's most popular work is his soundtrack to *Ladies in Lavender,* the 2004 movie, directed by Charles Dance and starring Dame Judi Dench and Dame Maggie Smith. He was previously the House Composer for the Royal Shakespeare Company, writing twenty scores for productions ranging from *Much Ado About Nothing* to *Cyrano de Bergerac.* His *Concerto for Piano and Orchestra* was commissioned by the Prince of Wales in memory of the Queen Mother, with the debut performance being given by the young Chinese superstar pianist, Lang Lang.

Check out: *Christmas Overture* – all of your favourite Christmas carols expertly stitched together in one place.

HANS ZIMMER (BORN 1957)

Another movie composer, Hans Zimmer is known principally for his soundtrack to *Gladiator,* along with a string of other movie scores. He had early success as the writer of television theme tunes.

Check out: *Mission Impossible | The Last Samurai | Rain Man | Pearl Harbour.*

THE NAME GAME

Stanley Myers' *Cavatina* is often known as 'the theme from *The Deer Hunter*'. But things could have been different. It would be fair also to call it 'the theme from *The Walking Stick*'. Myers originally wrote it for the 1971 film called *The Walking Stick* and simply reused it seven years later in *The Deer Hunter.*

DARIO MARIANELLI (BORN 1963)

He may have been born in the Italian city of Pisa, a city most famous for its leaning tower, but Dario Marianelli is no slouch when it comes to composing. With an awards cabinet that would put Manchester United to shame, he has been honoured by the Oscars, the Golden Globes, BAFTA and the Classical Brit Awards, to name but a few.

Check out: *Pride & Prejudice | Atonement | The Brothers Grimm | The Soloist.*

Well, I Never! Marianelli is now composing exclusive ringtones for Vertu, the eye-wateringly expensive mobile phone brand.

AN A TO Z OF LITTLE KNOWN COMPOSERS

Abaelardus	Nenna
Brod	Ostrcil
Cato	Pez
Damett	Queldryk
Eechaute	Ruffo
Facoli	Schop
Gehot	Titov
Hagg	Uttini
Ishchenko	Vitols
Jirko	Waelput
Kaski	Xyndas
Le Flem	Youll
Mossi	Zani

ONLINE PREMIERE

In 2009, the London Symphony Orchestra created the world's first collaborative online symphony orchestra, the YouTube Symphony, which made its debut at Carnegie Hall in New York on 15th April, 2009.

ROYAL ORCHESTRA

The Philharmonia Orchestra has only had 5 principal conductors in its 65 year history, the latest of whom is Esa-Pekka Salonen. The Prince of Wales is the Orchestra's Patron, but the royal connections don't stop there: the Indian Prince, the Maharajah of Mysore, was the Philharmonia's first president.

NEAR MISS

In 1912, the London Symphony Orchestra was the first British orchestra to visit the United States, only narrowly avoiding travelling on the *Titanic*.

LADIES FIRST

Originally set up in 1945 by the record company executive Walter Legge as a recording orchestra for EMI, the Philharmonia was the first London orchestra to admit female members.

WHO FOLLOWED WHOM?

Hildegard of Bingen .... 1098 – 1179
Guillaume de Machaut .... 1300 – 1377
John Dunstable .... 1390 – 1453
Guillaume Dufay .... 1397 – 1474
John Tavener .... 1490 – 1545
Thomas Tallis .... 1505 – 1585
Giovanni Pierluigi da Palestrina .... 1525 – 1594
William Byrd .... 1537 – 1623
Jacopo Peri .... 1561 – 1633
Claudio Monteverdi .... 1567 – 1643
Gregorio Allegri .... 1582 – 1652
Orlando Gibbons .... 1583 – 1625
Jean-Baptiste Lully .... 1632 – 1687
Marc-Antoine Charpentier .... 1643 – 1704
Arcangelo Corelli .... 1653 – 1713
Johann Pachelbel .... 1653 – 1706
Henry Purcell .... 1659 – 1695
Tomaso Albinoni .... 1671 – 1750
Antonio Vivaldi .... 1678 – 1741
Georg Philipp Telemann .... 1681 – 1767
Domenico Scarlatti .... 1685 – 1757
Johann Sebastian Bach .... 1685 – 1750
George Frideric Handel .... 1685 – 1759
Domenico Zipoli .... 1688 – 1726
Christoph Willibald von Gluck .... 1714 – 1787
Carl Philippe Emanuel Bach .... 1714 – 1788
Joseph Haydn .... 1732 – 1809
Johann Christian Bach .... 1735 – 1782
Karl Ditters von Dittersdorf .... 1739 – 1799
Luigi Boccherini .... 1743 – 1805
Antonio Salieri .... 1750 – 1825
Wolfgang Amadeus Mozart .... 1756 – 1791
Ludwig van Beethoven .... 1770 – 1827
Niccolò Paganini .... 1782 – 1840
Louis Spohr .... 1784 – 1859
Carl Maria von Weber .... 1786 – 1826
Gioachino Rossini .... 1792 – 1868
Franz Schubert .... 1797 – 1828

Gaetano Donizetti . . . . 1797 – 1848
Hector Berlioz . . . . 1803 – 1869
Johann Strauss Sr . . . . 1804 – 1849
Mikhail Glinka . . . . 1804 – 1857
Felix Mendelssohn . . . . .1809 – 1847
Frédéric Chopin . . . . 1810 – 1849
Robert Schumann . . . . 1810 – 1856
Franz Liszt . . . . 1811 – 1886
Giuseppe Verdi . . . . 1813 – 1901
Richard Wagner . . . . 1813 – 1883
Charles Gounod . . . . 1818 – 1893
Jacques Offenbach . . . . 1819 – 1880
César Franck . . . . 1822 – 1890
Anton Bruckner . . . . 1824 – 1896
Bedřich Smetana . . . . 1824 – 1884
Johann Strauss Jr . . . . 1825 – 1899
Alexander Borodin . . . . 1833 – 1887
Johannes Brahms . . . . 1833 – 1897
Camille Saint-Saëns . . . . 1835 – 1921
Léo Delibes . . . . 1836 – 1891
Georges Bizet . . . . 1838 – 1875
Max Bruch . . . . 1838 – 1920
Modest Mussorgsky . . . . 1838 – 1881
Peter Ilyich Tchaikovsky . . . . 1840 – 1893
Antonín Dvořák . . . . 1841 – 1904
Jules Massenet . . . . 1842 – 1912
Arthur Sullivan . . . . 1842 – 1900
Edvard Grieg . . . . 1843 – 1907
Nikolai Rimsky-Korsakov . . . . 1844 – 1908
Charles-Marie Widor . . . . 1844 – 1932
Gabriel Fauré . . . . 1845 – 1924
Hubert Parry . . . . 1848 – 1918
Leoš Janáček . . . . 1854 – 1928
Ruggero Leoncavallo . . . . 1857 – 1919
Edward Elgar . . . . 1857 – 1934
Giacomo Puccini . . . . 1858 – 1924
Gustav Mahler . . . . 1860 – 1911
Isaac Albéniz . . . . 1860 – 1909
Claude Debussy . . . . 1862 – 1918
Frederick Delius . . . . 1862 – 1934

Pietro Mascagni . . . . 1863 – 1945
Richard Strauss . . . . 1864 – 1949
Alexander Glazunov . . . . 1865 – 1936
Jean Sibelius . . . . 1865 – 1957
Erik Satie . . . . 1866 – 1925
Ralph Vaughan Williams . . . . 1872 – 1958
Sergei Rachmaninov . . . . 1873 – 1943
Gustav Holst . . . . 1874 – 1934
Arnold Schoenberg . . . . 1874 – 1951
Maurice Ravel . . . . 1875 – 1937
Béla Bartók . . . . 1881 – 1945
Igor Stravinsky . . . . 1882 – 1971
Sergei Prokofiev . . . . 1891 – 1953
Carl Orff . . . . 1895 – 1982
George Gershwin . . . . 1898 – 1937
Francis Poulenc . . . . 1899 – 1963
Aaron Copland . . . . 1900 – 1990
Joaquín Rodrigo . . . . 1901 – 1999
William Walton . . . . 1902 – 1983
Aram Khachaturian . . . . 1903 – 1978
Dmitri Shostakovich . . . . 1906 – 1975
Samuel Barber . . . . 1910 – 1981
John Cage . . . . 1912 – 1992
Benjamin Britten . . . . 1913 – 1976
Leonard Bernstein . . . . 1918 – 1990
Malcolm Arnold . . . . 1921 – 2006
John Williams . . . . 1932 –
Henryk Górecki . . . . 1933 –
John Barry . . . . 1933 –
Peter Maxwell Davies . . . . 1934 –
Arvo Pärt . . . . 1935 –
Philip Glass . . . . 1937 –
Jon Lord . . . . 1941 –
Paul McCartney . . . . 1942 –
Michael Nyman . . . . 1944 –
John Tavener . . . . 1944 –
Karl Jenkins . . . . 1944 –
John Rutter . . . . 1945 –
Howard Shore . . . . 1946 –
Jay Ungar . . . . 1946 –

Wilberforce knew somebody had detuned a string on his viola.
He just couldn't be sure which one.

175

THE CLASSIC FM HALL OF FAME

Each year since 1996, we have asked our listeners to vote for their favourite three classical works. We combine all of the votes into a Top 300. It's a living, breathing chart and so it changes each year as particular works come to prominence, or fall out of fashion. So, there is never really ever a single, definitive chart, rather a snapshot of classical music tastes at a given moment. This is the Top 300 from 2009:

1. Vaughan Williams: *The Lark Ascending*
2. Rachmaninov: *Piano Concerto No. 2*
3. Vaughan Williams: *Fantasia on a Theme by Thomas Tallis*
4. Beethoven: *Piano Concerto No. 5 ('Emperor')*
5. Beethoven: *Symphony No. 6 ('Pastoral')*
6. Mozart: *Clarinet Concerto*
7. Bruch: *Violin Concerto No. 1*
8. Elgar: *Cello Concerto*
9. Beethoven: *Symphony No. 9 ('Choral')*
10. Elgar: *Enigma Variations*
11. Pachelbel: *Canon in D*
12. Grieg: *Piano Concerto*
13. Jenkins: *The Armed Man 'A Mass for Peace'*
14. Saint-Saëns: *Symphony No.3 in C minor 'Organ'*
15. Barber: *Adagio for Strings*
16. Holst: *The Planets*
17. Tchaikovsky: *1812 Overture*
18. Rodrigo: *Concierto de Aranjuez*
19. Allegri: *Miserere*
20. Ungar: *The Ashokan Farewell*
21. Rachmaninov: *Symphony No.2*
22. Beethoven: *Symphony No.7*
23. Shostakovich: *Piano Concerto No.2*
24. Dvořák: *Symphony No.9 ('New World')*
25. Mozart: *Requiem*
26. Sibelius: *Finlandia*
27. Handel: *Messiah*
28. Mascagni: *Cavalleria Rusticana*
29. Gershwin: *Rhapsody in Blue*
30. Rachmaninov: *Rhapsody on a theme of Paganini*
31. Beethoven: *Symphony No. 5*
32. Shore: *Lord of the Rings*
33. Rimsky-Korsakov: *Scheherazade*
34. Vivaldi: *Four Seasons*
35. Mendelssohn: *Violin Concerto*
36. Handel: *Zadok the Priest*
37. Beethoven: *Piano Sonata No.14 'Moonlight'*
38. Fauré: *Requiem*
39. Bizet: *The Pearl Fishers*
40. Bach, J.S.: *Double Violin Concerto in D minor*
41. Rachmaninov: *Piano Concerto No.3*
42. Tchaikovsky: *Swan Lake*
43. Tchaikovsky: *Piano Concerto No.1*
44. Mozart: *Piano Concerto No.21*
45. Mahler: *Symphony No.5*
46. Debussy: *Suite Bergamasque*
47. Strauss, R.: *Four Last Songs*
48. Tchaikovsky: *Symphony No.6 ('Pathétique')*
49. Grieg: *Peer Gynt Suite*
50. Smetana: *Ma Vlast*
51. Vaughan Williams: *Five Variants of Dives and Lazarus*
52. Tchaikovsky: *Symphony No.5*
53. Mendelssohn: *Hebrides Overture*
54. Sibelius: *Karelia Suite*
55. Elgar: *Pomp and Circumstance Marches*
56. Butterworth: *The Banks of Green Willow*
57. Bach, J.S.: *Toccata and Fugue in D minor*
58. Hess: *Ladies in Lavender*

177

INDEX

180

181

ACKNOWLEDGEMENTS

We are greatly indebted to Mark Searle, Lorne Forsyth and Ellen Marshall at Elliott and Thompson for turning this book from dream to reality in a very short space of time. Our thanks also go to Andrew Hanley and David Bray for helping us along the way. We are also grateful to many of our colleagues at Classic FM for their suggestions and advice, especially Sam Jackson, Stuart Campbell, Richard Porter, Rupert Reid, Anne-Marie Minhall, Charlotte Rosier, Giles Pearman, Vicki Simpson and Emma Oxborrow.